AF664101

A Passage to India

Martin Sherman was born in Philadelphia, educated at Boston University and now lives in London. His plays include: *Passing By, Cracks* and *Rio Grande* (Playwrights Horizons, New York); *Bent* (Royal Court Theatre, London, 1979, subsequently West End and Broadway, where it received a Tony nomination for Best Play and won the Dramatist's Guild Hull-Warriner award). *Bent* has been performed in over thirty-five countries and was revived by the National Theatre in 1989. His other plays include *Messiah* (Hampstead Theatre and Aldwych, London, 1983); *When She Danced* (King's Head Theatre, London, 1988 and Gielgud, 1991); *A Madhouse in Goa* (Lyric Hammersmith and Apollo Theatre, London, 1989); *Some Sunny Day* (Hampstead Theatre, 1996); *Rose* (National Theatre, London, 1999) which received a Olivier nomination for Best Play and transferred to Broadway in 2000. His screenplays include: *The Clothes in the Wardrobe* (BBC Television, 1992; US title *The Summer House*, 1994); *Alive and Kicking*; *Bent* (1997); Franco Zefferelli's *Callas Forever* and *The Roman Spring of Mrs Stone.*

A Passage to India

[illegible]

[illegible]

E. M. Forster's

A Passage to India

adapted for the stage by

Martin Sherman

BLOOMSBURY
NEW DELHI • LONDON • OXFORD • NEW YORK • SYDNEY

First published in India 2017
First published 2002 by Methuen Publishing Limited

A Passage to India by E. M. Forster ©
The Provost and Scholars of King's College, Cambridge 1924, 1979.

A Passage to India – play © The Provost and Scholars of Kings College,
Cambridge and Martin Sherman 2002.

Martin Sherman has asserted his right under the Copyright,
Designs and Patents Act, 1988, to be identified as author of this work.

Bloomsbury Methuen Drama
An imprint of Bloomsbury Publishing Plc
Bloomsbury is a registered trade mark of Bloomsbury Publishing Plc
This edition published with permission from Bloomsbury Publishing Plc
50 Bedford Square, London WC1B 3DP

All rights reserved. No part of this publication may be reproduced or transmitted in any form or by any means, electronic or mechanical, including photocopying, recording, or any information storage or retrieval system, without prior permission in writing from the publishers.

No responsibility for loss caused to any individual or organization acting on or refraining from action as a result of the material in this publication can be accepted by Bloomsbury or the author.

All rights whatsoever in this play are strictly reserved and application for performance etc. should be made before rehearsals by professionals and by amateurs to Casarotto Ramsay & Associates Ltd, Waverley House, 7–12 Noel Street, London W1F 8GQ Mail to: agents@casarotto.co.uk. No performance may be given unless a licence has been obtained.

No rights in incidental music or songs contained in the work are hereby granted and performance rights for any performance/presentation whatsoever must be obtained from the respective copyright owners.

Visit www.bloomsbury.com to find out more about our authors and their books
You will find extracts, author interviews, author events and you can sign up for newsletters to be the first to hear about our latest releases and special offers.

British Library Cataloguing-in-Publication Data
A catalogue record for this book is available from the British Library.
Library of Congress Cataloging-in-Publication Data
A catalog record for this book is available from the Library of Congress

ISBN: 978 93 86349 50 7
10 9 8 7 6 5 4 3
For sale in the Indian subcontinent only

Bloomsbury Publishing India Pvt. Ltd
Second Floor, Building No. 4
DDA Complex LSC, Pocket C – 6 & 7
Vasant Kunj, New Delhi 110070
www.bloomsbury.com

Printed and bound in India by Replika Press Pvt. Ltd.

for Nancy Meckler

A Passage to India premiered at the Richmond Theatre, Surrey, on 18 September 2002. The cast was as follows:

Dr Aziz	Paul Bazeley
Adela Quested	Penny Laden
Mahmoud Ali **Tiger**	Nicholas Khan
Cyril Fielding	Ian Gelder
Miss Derek **Mrs Turton**	Priyanga Elan
Mrs Moore	Susan Engel
Professor Narayan **Godbole** **Burton**	Aaron Neil
Turton **McBryde**	Geoffrey Beevers
Ronny Heaslop **Ralph**	Guy Lankester
Rafi/Das	Daniel Hope
Hamidullah	Antony Bunsee

Director Nancy Meckler
Designer Niki Turner
Lighting Designer Chris Davey
Composer Peter Salem

A Passage to India was commissioned by Shared Experience, a company that unites both physical and text-based theatre, creating an individual and distinctive performance style. This meant I could dare to imagine the most complicated and sometimes spectacular scenes in the knowledge that the director, Nancy Meckler, would translate them into a visual language at once simple and evocative. Thus the stage directions in this text are not to be taken literally, but instead as a blueprint for a passage into theatrical possibility.

Act One

Professor Narayan Godbole *addresses the audience. He is sitting on strip of carpet. He is barefoot and in white. He wears a pale-blue turban.*

Godbole Long before Dr Aziz settled in our state, in Mau, another young Mohammedan lived here.

A beautiful **Young Man** *stands in a ray of light. He is naked except for a loincloth. He is in front of a house. An older woman – his* **Mother** *– comes out of the house. She looks at him sternly.*

Godbole One day his mother said to him – free the prisoners. So he took a sword and went up to the fort. He unlocked a door and the prisoners streamed out and resumed their former occupations, but the police were too much annoyed and cut off the young man's head.

The **Young Man**, *the* **Prisoners**, *the* **Police** *act out the story as* **Godbole** *relates it.*

Godbole Ignoring its absence he made his way over the rocks that separated the fort and the town, killing policemen as he went, and fell outside his mother's house.

The **Young Man** *stretches the sword out to his* **Mother** *and dies.*

Godbole Consequently, there are two shrines to that young man today, here in our town – that of the Head above, and that of the Body below . . .

Villagers *turn the* **Young Man**'*s body and then his head into two separate shrines, which stand on either side of the stage for the rest of the play.*

Godbole . . . and although ours is a Hindu state, they are worshipped by all who live here. The Shrine of the Body actually lies in Dr Aziz's garden. The Shrine of the Head is a short walk down. He takes his children there sometimes. Shall I tell you about Dr Aziz?

Pause.

Actually, the young man – he of the head and the body – is a saint, not a god. God is not born yet. Well, He will be, tonight, in our yearly festival. He has also been born centuries ago, nor can He ever be born, because He is the Lord of the Universe, who transcends human processes. He is, was not, is not, was. He stands with me now.

He rises and stands on the carpet. he begins to sing.

Radhakrishna, Radhkrishna,
Radhakrishna, Radhkrishna,
Krisnanradha, Krisnanradha,
Radhakrishna, Radhkrishna . . .

He plays a cymbal. Inscriptions appear on banners. One of them reads GOD SI LOVE. **Godbole** *looks up at the banner.*

Not everyone here can spell. And yet. God Si Love. Is that the final message of India? (*Pause.*) Who was I telling you about? Dr Aziz. Yes. Although he is a follower of Islam, he has settled here with his children – two years now. Dr Aziz came to us from Chandrapore. As did I. (*Pause.*) I am flooded with memories now, but they are meaningless.
I think of an old woman I met in Chandrapore. Shall I tell you about her? Memories occur. I cannot stop them.
I remember a wasp. Where did I see it? Perhaps on a stone. The stone and the wasp – and the old woman – I love equally. For I imitate God.

Godbole*'s* **Students** – *a* **Choir** – *appear by the side of the carpet. They sing along with him.*

Godbole *and* **Choir**

Radhakrishna Radhakrishna,
Radhakrishna Radhakrishna . . .

The music intensifies. There is noise now. Distant thunder. Cymbals clashing. And incense. **Godbole** *begins to dance on the carpet.*

Suddenly **Dr Aziz** *appears. He is handsome, compact, wiry, volatile.*

Godbole *stops.*

Godbole Ah. Dr Aziz. We practise.

Aziz Practise?

Godbole Rehearse. For tonight's ceremony – the birth of our God. It is the main event of our religious year. And within it I rediscover my spirit. Well. You are perhaps waiting to greet our guest.

Aziz Guest?

Godbole He has arrived at the European guest house perhaps – at least possibly.

Aziz Who?

Godbole Did I not tell you? My former superior from Chandrapore.

Aziz Fielding?

Godbole He is on an inspection tour of Central India. He is with his wife and her brother. Surely I mentioned it.

Aziz I have no desire to see Fielding. Or his wife.

Aziz *walks off.*

Godbole *returns to the audience, as if the interruption had not occurred.*

Godbole I saw the old woman once again. The wasp as well. Now I leave. (*Pause.*) One old Englishwoman and one little wasp. It does not seem much; still, it is more than I am myself.

Godbole *leaves.*

Aziz *sits by the Shrine of the Body. He looks at the sky. Distant thunder. Suddenly two* **Climbers** *enter, or rather, run on pursued by bees. They are* **Fielding**, *an untidy, greying man – and a* **Boy**, *aged eighteen.* **Aziz** *is agitated by the sight of* **Fielding** *and starts to leave, but he is also amused by the bee attack. Finally he has to speak.*

Aziz Hello, gentlemen, are you in trouble?

Boy I've been stung.

Aziz Lie down in a pool of water, my dear sir. Here are plenty. Don't come near me . . . I can't control them; they are State bees; complain to His Highness of their behaviour.

The bees fly away.

Aziz They are gone now, at any rate. (*Goes to* **Boy**; *the* **Boy** *instinctively pulls away from him.*) Come, come – I am a doctor.

Fielding (*smiles*) A very fine doctor.

Aziz *ignores him; the* **Boy** *gives* **Aziz** *his hand and* **Aziz** *pulls a couple of stings out of the* **Boy***'s wrist.*

Fielding How do you do, Aziz, after all this time? (**Aziz** *doesn't answer.*) How goes it, Aziz?

Aziz In my usual health.

Pause.

Fielding I have missed you, Aziz.

Aziz *stares at him, then turns away.*

Aziz Do not trouble me here. That is all I ask. I do not want you.

Fielding Aziz . . .

Aziz I do not want any of you in my private life. I have forgotten all of you. You no longer exist.

A mist envelops **Aziz** *and the two* **Men**. *Mau disappears.*

A **Woman** (**Adela**) *appears in the mist, her face scratched, her clothes torn, her eyes dazed, and then she too disappears.*

A mosque appears.

Chandrapore. Two years earlier.

Aziz *walks into the mosque. A beautiful moonlit night. He sits on a low wall. He can hear sounds in the night – on the right, an amateur* *orchestra from the English club; elsewhere, Hindus drumming; somewhere else, mourners bewailing a corpse. An owl.*

Suddenly there is movement. The mosque seems to quiver. An **Englishwoman** *steps out into the moonlight, but her face is hidden.* **Aziz** *is angry.*

Englishwoman Oh! Oh!

Aziz Madame, this is a mosque, you have no right here at all; you should have taken off your shoes; this is a holy place for Moslems.

Englishwoman I have taken them off.

Aziz You have?

Englishwoman I left them at the entrance.

Aziz Then I ask your pardon.

The **Englishwoman**, *still startled, moves away.*

Aziz I am truly sorry for speaking.

Englishwoman Yes, I am right, was I not? If I remove my shoes I am allowed?

Aziz Of course, but so few ladies take the trouble, especially if thinking no one is there to see you.

Englishwoman That makes no difference. God is here.

Aziz Madame!

Englishwoman Please let me go.

Aziz Can I do you some service – now or at any time?

Englishwoman No, thank you, really none – goodnight.

Aziz May I know your name?

Englishwoman Mrs Moore.

He moves towards her. She steps out of the shadows. We see that she is old; her voice deceived him.

Aziz Mrs Moore, I am afraid I startled you. I shall tell our community – my friends – about you. That God is here – very good, very fine indeed. I think that you are newly arrived in India.

Mrs Moore Yes – how did you know?

Aziz By the way you address me. Can I call you a carriage?

Mrs Moore I have only come from the club. They are doing a play that I have seen in London and it was so hot . . .

Aziz I think you ought not to walk at night alone, Mrs Moore. There are bad characters about and leopards may come across from the Marabar Hills. Snakes also.

Mrs Moore But you walk about yourself.

Aziz Oh, I am used to it.

Mrs Moore Used to snakes?

Aziz I'm a doctor. Snakes don't dare bite me.

They laugh and sit down, side by side in the entrance, and slip on their evening shoes.

May I ask you a question now? Why ever do you come to Chandrapore?

Mrs Moore I have escorted a young lady here from England. She and my son contemplate marriage. But they are cautious. My son is the City Magistrate here.

Aziz Oh no, excuse me, that is quite impossible. Our City Magistrate's name is Mr Heaslop.

Mrs Moore He's my son all the same. I was married twice.

Aziz Yes, now I see, and your first husband died.

Mrs Moore He did, and so did my second husband.

Aziz And is the City Magistrate the entire of your family now?

Mrs Moore No, there are the young ones from my second marriage, Ralph and Stella, in England.

Aziz Mrs Moore, this is all extremely strange, because like yourself, I have also two sons and a daughter. And their mother, my wife, has also died. We are in the same box.

Mrs Moore And your children? . . .

Aziz They are most comfortably with my wife's mother. I can see them whenever I like. They are such very, very small children.

Mrs Moore What are their names? Not also Ronny, Ralph and Stella surely?

Aziz No indeed. How funny it sounds. Their names are quite different and will surprise you. Listen, please. I am about to tell you my children's names. The first is called Ahmed, the second is called Karim, the third – she is the eldest – Jamila. Three children are enough. Do you not agree?

Mrs Moore I do.

They are both silent for a moment.

Aziz Would you care to see over the Lintel hospital one morning? I have nothing else to offer at Chandrapore.

Mrs Moore Thank you, I have seen it already, or I should like to have come with you very much.

Aziz I suppose my superior at the hospital, Major Callender, took you.

Mrs Moore Yes, and Mrs Callender.

Aziz Ah. A very charming lady.

Mrs Moore Possibly, when one knows her better.

Aziz What? What? You didn't like her?

Mrs Moore She was certainly intending to be kind, but I did not find her exactly charming.

Aziz Charming! She has just taken my tonga without my permission – do you call that being charming? And her husband, my superior at the hospital, interrupts me night after night from where I am dining with my friends, saying I must come to him at once, and I go at once, breaking up a most pleasant entertainment, and he is not there and not even a message, and then his wife runs past me, as I say, without even an acknowledgement, and takes my carriage. Is this charming? . . . Forgive me, my tongue runs ahead of my brain sometimes. My friends say I talk too much. But I think you understand me, you know what I feel. Oh, if others resembled you.

Mrs Moore I don't think I do understand people very well. I only know whether I like – or dislike – them.

Aziz Ah. (*Smiles.*) Then you are an Oriental.

She smiles back.

Ronny Heaslop*'s bungalow.* **Mrs Moore** *is knitting.* **Adela Quested** *bursts into the room. She is tremulous, in her late twenties.*

Adela I want to see the *real* India.

Mrs Moore I want to see it too and only wish we could. Apparently the Chief Administrator, Mr Turton, and his wife will arrange something for next Tuesday.

Adela It'll end up in an elephant ride, it always does. I really didn't come up here to see *elephants*!

Mrs Moore (*amused*) There are quite a few cows as well.

Adela I thought I would go out of my mind this evening at the club. That dreadful play, *Cousin Kate.* I saw it last year in London with my play discussion group, and we had nothing to discuss – there were no *issues* involved. And then the meal after – sardines on toast, peas, cutlets, trifle, we might as well have been in Surrey. There were no spices. I long for – yes, that's it – *flavour*! I was desperate to leave. As indeed you seem to have done. Where were you off to? Did you succeed in catching the moon in the Ganges?

Mrs Moore I went to the mosque, but I did not catch the moon.

Ronny *enters. He is in his early thirties.*

Ronny Adela, have a drink? Mother, a drink?

Mrs Moore No thank you, dear.

Adela I was just saying, Ronny, that I'd like to see the real India.

Ronny Fielding says one can only see the real India by seeing Indians. What a peculiar man he is.

Mrs Moore Who is, dear?

Ronny Fielding, the schoolmaster.

Adela But excepting my own servant, whom I rather distrust, I've scarcely spoken to an Indian since landing. Nor have I seen anything other than the club. Your mother has at least been to a mosque.

Ronny Have you?

Mrs Moore Yes, tonight.

Ronny When?

Mrs Moore Whilst the play was on.

Ronny But Mother, you can't do that sort of thing.

Mrs Moore Can't Mother?

Ronny No, really not in this country. It's not done. There's the danger from snakes for one thing.

Mrs Moore Ah yes, so the young man there said.

Adela This sounds very romantic. You met a young man in a mosque and only now let me know? Was he nice?

Mrs Moore Very nice.

Ronny Who was he?

Mrs Moore A doctor. I don't know his name.

Ronny A doctor? I know of no young doctor in Chandrapore.

Mrs Moore We had a lovely conversation. He told me about his children and then he walked me back to the club. He knows you.

Ronny I wish you had pointed him out to me. I can't make out who he is.

Mrs Moore He didn't come into the club. He said he wasn't allowed to.

Ronny Oh, good gracious! Not a Mohammedan? Why ever didn't you tell me you'd been talking to a native.

Adela A Mohammedan! How perfectly magnificent. Ronny, isn't that like your mother? While we talk about seeing the real India, she goes and sees it and then forgets she's seen it.

Ronny What was he doing there himself at that time of night?

Adela Perhaps it was prayer time.

Ronny No, it's not their prayer time. You must tell me more about this native.

Mrs Moore I believe he's connected to the hospital.

Ronny Oh. Oh yes. Chap's name is Aziz. He's quite all right. Nothing against him at all.

Mrs Moore Aziz! What a charming name!

Ronny So you and he had a talk. Did you gather he was well-disposed? Did he seem to tolerate us – the brutal conqueror, that sort of thing?

Mrs Moore Oh yes, I think so, except the Callenders – he doesn't care for the Callenders at all.

Ronny Oh, so he told you that, did he? The Major will be interested.

Mrs Moore Ronny, you're never going to pass it on to Major Callender!

Ronny Yes, Mother, I must in fact.

Mrs Moore But my dear boy – a private conversation!

Ronny Nothing's private in India. Aziz knew that when he spoke out, so don't you worry. He had some motive in what he said.

Mrs Moore You never used to judge people like this at home.

Ronny India isn't home.

Mrs Moore You really must not hand on to Major Callender anything I have told you about Dr Aziz.

Adela No, Ronny, you mustn't. He sounds like a lovely chap. And your mother is quite right . . . a private conversation is sacrosanct.

Ronny (*smiles*) Lovely word. But it doesn't apply out here. You are quite unaware of the social mores of this country.

Adela I think not. I've read quite a lot about India. I've attended several lectures on the subject. I'm not uninformed.

Ronny I didn't mean to suggest you were.

Mrs Moore Adela, dear, might you fetch my playing cards?

Adela Yes, what a good idea. There really doesn't seem to be any other way to pass the time.

Adela *leaves the room.*

Ronny I do wish you would not talk about this Aziz fellow to Adela.

Mrs Moore Not talk about him. Why?

Ronny I don't want Adela to be worried.

Mrs Moore Why on earth should that worry her? At any rate, she came out here to be worried. That's why she's here. She discussed it all on the boat. She knows you in play, as she put it, but not in work, and she felt she must come and look around before she decides – and before you decided. She is being very fair-minded.

Ronny (*dejected*) I know.

Mrs Moore But, dear, I did want to have this moment to suggest that you ought to be more alone with her than you are.

Ronny Yes, perhaps, but then people'd talk.

Mrs Moore Well, let them.

Ronny It's difficult. People are odd out here. They notice everything until they're perfectly sure that you're their sort.

Mrs Moore I don't think Adela'll ever be quite their sort – she's much too individual.

Ronny I know, that's so remarkable about her. I suppose nothing's on her mind?

Mrs Moore Ask her yourself, my dear boy.

Ronny But you can sense things.

Mrs Moore Perhaps some of the people she's met at the club are getting on her nerves; they make unpleasant comments about the Indians, you see.

Ronny How like a woman to worry over a side issue. We're not here to make pleasant comments. Are we all supposed to lose our ability to do good in this country because our behaviour isn't always pleasant? I spend my days in court trying to decide which of two untrue accounts is less untrue, trying to protect the weak against the less weak, indeed, trying to dispense justice and keep the peace, and if along the way I or my associates are not pleasant it is because we have something far more important to do.

Mrs Moore I disagree. The English *are* out here to be pleasant.

Ronny How do you make that out, Mother?

Mrs Moore Because India is part of the earth. And God has put us on earth in order to be pleasant to each other. God . . . is . . . love.

Ronny Yes. I quite see that. (*Pause.*) You must tell me if you're feeling unwell.

Mrs Moore Why is that?

Ronny When you go all religious, it's often a symptom of bad health.

Mrs Moore (*laughs*) I should not have mentioned God. I'm sorry. But He's difficult to avoid as one grows older. He's been constantly in my thoughts since I entered this country, though oddly enough, He satisfies me less. It's as though there's an arch, and beyond that another arch, and beyond that – silence. Do you understand?

He stares at her. He doesn't.

Adela *returns with playing cards.*

Adela But Ronny, I was thinking, why *can't* we meet some Indians? It's ridiculous to be in India and not to see Indians – really, it's as simple as that.

Mrs Moore *shoots a knowing look at* **Ronny**.

Ronny Oh dear. (*Pause.*) Would you like a bridge party?

Adela You mean you would like us to play cards with them. (*Sits at the card table with* **Mrs Moore**.)

Ronny No, our civil administrator, Mr Turton, has concocted this idea of bridge parties – a party to bridge the gulf between East and West. The expression is his own invention.

Adela I only want to meet those Indians you come across socially – as your friends.

Ronny Well, we don't come across them socially except at an event like a . . .

Mrs Moore Bridge party.

Ronny Yes, Mother.

Adela I would so like that, Ronny. (*Pats his hand.*) You are really very thoughtful.

Ronny Thank you, Adela. (*An uncomfortable pause.*) I think perhaps I should retire.

He kisses his mother on her forehead, then notices something on the side of her chair, and picks up a brochure which he raises above his head, as if to strike.

Mrs Moore Good heavens. What is it?

Ronny Just a wasp.

Mrs Moore No, no, leave it. Please.

Ronny *lowers the brochure.* **Mrs Moore** *squeezes his hand.*

Mrs Moore Goodnight.

Ronny *bows to* **Adela**.

Ronny Adela.

Adela Ronny.

Ronny *leaves.*

Mrs Moore *looks at the wasp on the arm of her chair.*

Mrs Moore Pretty dear.

Aziz *runs on with a bicycle which he places on the ground. He rushes into* **Hamidullah***'s house.*

Aziz Hamidullah! Hamidullah! Am I late?

He finds **Hamidullah** *and* **Mahmoud Ali**, *both dressed in orthodox Moslem clothing, on the veranda, sitting in front of a hookah.*

Hamidullah Do not apologise. You are always late.

Aziz But it has been a difficult day. One ruptured appendix, one hernia . . .

Hamidullah Please, spare us the details. We do not entertain you with the minutiae of our day in the law courts.

Aziz Has Mahmoud Ali eaten all the food? If so I go elsewhere. Mr Mahmoud Ali, how are you?

Mahmoud Ali Thank you, Dr Aziz, I am dying.

Aziz Dying before dinner? Oh, poor Mahmoud Ali.

Hamidullah Aziz, don't chatter. We are having an important talk. We are discussing whether or not it is possible to be friends with an Englishman. I have received an invitation, as has Mahmoud Ali, as I'm sure you have, to join Mr Turton in the garden of the club between the hours of five and seven on Tuesday.

Aziz Ah, yes. Those are busy hours for me at the hospital. I doubt that I will attend.

Hamidullah Did you know that when Turton first came out to assume his post, I drove with him in his carriage – oh yes, Turton! We were quite intimate. He showed me his stamp collection.

Mahmoud Ali Now he would expect you to steal it.

Hamidullah They all become exactly the same. I give any Englishman two years. And I give any Englishwoman two months. Do you not agree with me?

Mahmoud Ali I do not. I find them not the same at all. That new magistrate mumbles, for instance. Whereas Turton talks distinctly. If you study them carefully, you can spot these differences. Mr Turton pretends towards integrity, while his wife quite openly takes bribes.

Hamidullah Bribes?

Mahmoud Ali Did you not know that when the canal scheme was proposed, some raja or other gave her a sewing machine in solid gold so that the water should run through his state.

Hamidullah And does it?

Mahmoud Ali Of course not. That is where Mrs Turton is so skilful. When we blacks take bribes, we perform what we are bribed to perform. The English take bribes but then do nothing. I admire them.

Aziz Mrs Turton, to be quite candid, had a beautifully formed gall bladder.

They laugh. **Aziz** *passes the hookah to* **Hamidullah**.

Hamidullah You are generous about our English friends, Aziz; indeed you have a tenderness for most everyone . . .

Aziz Not Major Callender and his wife.

Hamidullah The Callenders excepted.

Aziz Because I know at the bottom of my heart that the English cannot help being so cold and odd. It is not their fault. They were created that way. I object only to the time we spend talking about them. We could instead be reciting poems. Listen . . .

He recites a Persian poem. He is in love with the poem; the words sing on his lips.

Hamidullah *and* **Mahmoud Ali** *listen.* **Aziz** *finishes. They are all in a stupor. There is a sense of perfect happiness.*

Aziz And this . . .

He recites another poem. The hookah is passed.

Hamidullah (*in a trance*) Words, words . . .

Aziz I breathe them like the night air. . .

Mahmoud Ali The poets, Hafiz, Hali, Iqbal . . .

Hamidullah A hundred languages. A hundred Indias . . .

Aziz No, tonight there is only one India – my own . . . (*He smiles in satisfaction.*)

The bridge party.

The club lawn. **Mr** *and* **Mrs Turton, Major Callender**, *and* **Mr Burton** *stand drinking tea on one side of the lawn, surrounded by other* **Members** *of the club.* **Ronny** *is with them, and an extremely awkward* **Adela** *and* **Mrs Moore**. *The* **Indians** *stand on the other side of the lawn, but we cannot see them. The* **English** *stare out at the audience as if they were looking at the* **Indians**. *There is no effort to communicate.*

Ronny (*to* **Turton**) It was very kind of you to arrange this party, sir.

Turton It's a pleasure, my boy.

Ronny (*to* **Adela**) Of course, the truth is that no one who's here matters; those who matter don't come. Isn't that so, Mrs Turton?

Mrs Turton Absolutely true. If only one could avoid an afternoon like this.

Turton (*looking across to the* **Indians**) Well, well . . . who have we so far? Hmm. Much as one expected. We know why that one's here – over that contract, and next to him is the astrologer who wants to bypass the municipal building regulations, and over there that Parsee with the family dispute . . . rather the turnout one expected. No surprises. Hello! What's this? One of them has driven his carriage into our hollyhocks. Pulled his horse's left rein when he meant the right. All as usual.

Mrs Turton They ought never to have been allowed to drive in; it's so bad for them.

Burton Why they come at all I don't know. They hate it as much as we do.

Turton (*to* **Adela**) Aside from a few broken blossoms, Miss Quested, it's hardly picturesque, I'm afraid.

Adela Everyone seems so pleasant.

Mrs Turton Natives don't respect one any the more after meeting one, you know. I was a nurse before my marriage and came across them a great deal, so I know. One has to stay firmly aloof.

Adela Even from one's patients?

Burton The kindest thing one can do to a native is to let him die.

Mrs Moore And then if he goes to heaven?

Major Callender He can go where he likes as long as he doesn't come near me.

Mrs Turton I take your point about heaven. It's made me think.

Mrs Moore *Has* it?

Mrs Turton Yes. And that is why I am against missionaries.

Adela Well, I think instead of standing around staring at them, we should introduce ourselves. I notice that the schoolmaster has already done so. Are you coming, Mrs Moore?

Mrs Moore With pleasure.

Adela *and* **Mrs Moore** *march off, followed by an embarrassed* **Ronny**.

Mrs Turton Miss Quested, what a name! I hope she hasn't been brought out to marry nice little Heaslop. It seems she comes from Hampstead. Mixes with a literary set.

Major Callender Oh dear, oh dear. I say, she's talking to quite a few of them, as is that schoolmaster.

Turton Fielding's quite a decent chap, actually. (*Indicates with a shake of his head that he sees* **Fielding** *mixing with the* **Indians**.)

Mrs Turton Fielding! He's not pukka, never will be. *He* should marry Miss Quested.

Major Callender They seem to be talking to most anyone.

Turton Right. Time to do our duty. To work, Mary, to work!

Mrs Turton What do you want me to do? Oh, those purdah women! I never thought any would come. Oh dear!

Turton Come along, Mary, get it over.

The **English** *turn around and are transformed into the* **Indians**, *talking in a crowd to* **Adela** *and* **Mrs Moore**.

Mrs Moore (*to an Indian woman,* **Mrs Bhattacharya**) I'm so sorry we don't speak your language . . .

Mrs Bhattacharya We speak a little of yours.

Adela How lovely.

Indian Man Eastbourne. Piccadilly. High Park Corner.

Mrs Bhattacharya Some of us a little more, some a little less. (*They laugh.*)

Adela *and* **Mrs Moore** *move with the* **Indians** *in a circle;* **Fielding** *is in a concurrent one. Chatter. The sun is blazing.*

Adela *is feeling the heat. Suddenly everything and everyone around her seems to fade. Reality disappears. It is dark and frightening.*

And then, just as suddenly, she snaps back, and it is light. She is facing hills that lie in the distance. She is alone, except for **Fielding**, *who is standing behind her.*

Fielding Those are the Marabar Hills.

Adela They look so close.

Fielding Far away, actually.

Adela Really?

Fielding I promise.

Adela They seem so peaceful.

Fielding (*holds out his hand*) Cyril Fielding.

Adela (*shaking his hand*) Adela Quested. You're the schoolmaster. I've heard about you.

Fielding (*smiles*) Yes. (*Pause.*) I'm afraid sunsets are very swift in the tropics.

Adela The bridge party hasn't been very successful, has it?

Fielding Well, you and Mrs Moore were not a failure. You actually broke quite a few conventions – you were friendly and polite – and our guests were very impressed. As was I.

Adela You circulated freely as well.

Fielding Yes, and it displeases some, but I can't be sacked from my job because my job is education. (*Pause.*) I'm rather a hermit, you know.

Adela Much the best thing to be in this place.

Fielding I don't get up too much to the club.

Adela And we never get down from it. (*Pause.*) I can see what a life is like out here. Looking into the club every evening, then driving home to dress. Seeing the Turtons and the Callenders and the McBrydes. Inviting them and being invited by them. A life. (*Pause.*) While India slides by unnoticed.

Fielding Then I would like very much to invite you and Mrs Moore to tea. And perhaps a few Indians as well.

Adela Oh, I would like that and so too would Mrs Moore, I know.

Fielding Do you care about Indian music? There is an old professor down at the college who sings.

Adela Oh, just what we would want to hear. And do you know Dr Aziz?

Fielding I know all about him. I don't know him. Would you like him asked too?

Adela Mrs Moore says he is so nice.

Fielding Very well, Miss Quested. Shall we plan on Thursday?

She turns to view the hills.

Godbole, *holding an invitation.*

Godbole I chose a purple turban. It was important to consider the colour. A coat, of course, a waistcoat, dhoti, and socks with a special design – clocks. Purple clocks. They created the appearance of harmony. Or of time standing still. (*He looks at the invitation again.*)

Aziz *is also reading an invitation. He takes off his doctor's uniform and puts on regular dress. He combs his hair. He is beside himself with excitement.*

Aziz *arrives at* **Fielding***'s house.*

Fielding *is inside, dressing after a bath. His* **Servant** *announces:*

Servant Dr Aziz.

Aziz *enters the living room. He cannot see* **Fielding** *who is in his dressing room.*

Fielding Please make yourself at home.

Aziz May I really, Mr Fielding? It's very good of you. I like unconventional behaviour so extremely. The fact is I have long wanted to meet you – I have heard so much about your warm heart. But where is one to meet in a wretched hole like Chandrapore? (*Walks close to the partition.*) When I was greener here, I'll tell you what; I used to wish you to fall ill so we could meet that way. Then we would have had jolly talks for you are a celebrated student of Persian poetry.

Fielding You know me by sight, then?

Aziz Of course, of course. You know me?

Fielding I know you very well by name.

Aziz I say, Mr Fielding.

Fielding Yes?

Aziz Guess what I look like before you come out. That will be a kind of game.

Fielding *is able to glimpse an image – or a shadow of* **Aziz** *– through the partition.*

Fielding You have a slim build.

Aziz Jolly good. What next? Do I have a venerable white beard?

Fielding Blast!

Aziz Anything wrong?

Fielding I've stamped on my last collar stud.

Aziz Take mine, take mine.

Fielding Have you a spare one?

Aziz Yes, yes, one minute.

Fielding Not if you're wearing it yourself.

Aziz No, no, one in my pocket.

Aziz *moves to the side and wrenches off his collar. He pulls a gold stud out of the back of his collar.*

Aziz Here it is.

Fielding Come in with it if you don't mind the unconventionality.

Aziz (*replaces his collar*) One minute again.

Aziz *walks into the other room and hands* **Fielding** *the stud.*

Fielding Many thanks.

They shake hands, smiling. **Aziz** *looks around the room.*

Aziz But I always thought that Englishmen kept their rooms so tidy. It seems this is not so. Everything arranged coldly on shelves is what I imagined. Is the stud going to go in?

Fielding I have my doubts.

Aziz Let me . . . I see . . . the hole is small..

Fielding Why in hell does one wear collars at all?

Aziz We wear them to pass the police.

Fielding What's that?

Aziz If I'm biking in English dress they take no notice. When I wear a fez they pull me over. Hooray! She's gone in! Sometimes I shut my eyes and dream I have splendid clothes and am riding into battle behind Alamgir.

Fielding Ah, Alamgir.

Aziz Must not India have been beautiful then with the Mogul Empire at its height and Alamgir reigning at Delhi upon the Peacock Throne?

Aziz *recites a Persian poem.* **Adela** *and* **Mrs Moore** *enter as he is reciting.* **Adela** *looks at* **Aziz**, *eyes wide, drinking in the poem.* **Fielding** *leads them to their seats.* **Adela** *now closes her eyes and* *lets the words drift over her. Persian music is heard.* **Godbole** *interrupts her reverie, walking through the centre, carrying a tea tray.*

The music has disappeared. They are seated now. **Fielding, Aziz, Adela** *and* **Mrs Moore** *drinking tea.* **Godbole** *takes his tea from a low table placed slightly behind him, to which he stretches back. He eats and smiles, eats and smiles, and says nothing. They are smoking.* **Aziz** *has been talking a blue streak.*

Aziz You remember the water by our mosque, Mrs Moore? It comes down from the mosque to this very garden and fills the tank outside – a skilful arrangement of the emperors. They stopped here going down into Bengal. They loved water. Wherever they went they created fountains, gardens, hammans.

Mrs Moore But how does the water gravitate uphill?

Aziz (*stumped, for his facts are incorrect*) A mystery.

Adela I do so hate mysteries.

Mrs Moore I like mysteries. But I rather dislike muddles.

Fielding A mystery is a muddle.

Mrs Moore Oh, do you think so, Mr Fielding?

Fielding A mystery is only a high-sounding term for a muddle. Aziz and I know well that India is a muddle.

Adela Oh, but a beautiful one, I imagine.

Aziz Why not settle altogether in India?

Adela No, I'm afraid I can't do that.

Aziz But you are not leaving us so soon?

Adela (*flustered*) Oh no . . . I didn't mean that exactly.

Aziz Visitors like you are too rare.

Adela We've seen so little.

Fielding Perhaps the ladies would like to view the college grounds.

Mrs Moore I'd be delighted to. May we?

Everyone rises except for **Godbole** *who is finishing a banana.*

Mrs Moore Don't you come too, Adela; you dislike institutions.

Adela Yes, that is so.

Adela *sits again.* **Mrs Moore** *and* **Fielding** *walk out through the garden.* **Aziz** *is disconcerted at being alone with* **Adela** *and* **Godbole**.

Aziz May I offer you . . . (*Holds out cigarettes.*)

Adela (*takes one*) Oh yes, thank you . . .

An awkward silence, as he lights her cigarette. They smoke.

Aziz Miss Quested, Professor Godbole brought delicious sweets. You must try them. They will give you a real Indian treat. Ah, in my poor position I can give you nothing. No – no – that is not true. I hereby invite you all to see me in the Marabar Caves. Yes!

Adela I shall be delighted.

Aziz (*surprised*) Oh. (*Pause.*) Unless you have visited them before?

Adela No, I've not even heard of them.

Aziz Not heard of them? The Marabar Caves in the Marabar Hills?

Adela We hear nothing interesting up at the club. Tell me everything you will, or I shall never understand India. What are these caves?

Aziz Actually, I've not been there myself. I've always been meaning to go but work has prevented me.

Adela Are they large caves?

Aziz *hesitates – he hasn't a clue.* **Godbole** *looks up.*

Godbole No, not large.

Adela Do describe them, Professor Godbole,

Godbole It will be a great honour. (*Draws up his chair.*) There is an entrance in the rock, where you enter. (*Pause.*)

Adela Yes?

Godbole And through the entrance is the cave.

Adela Something like the caves at Elefanta?

Godbole Oh no, not at all. At Elefanta there are sculptures of Siva and Parvati. There are no sculptures at all at Marabar.

Aziz They are immensely holy, no doubt.

Godbole Oh no, oh no.

Aziz Still they are ornamented in some way.

Godbole Oh no.

Aziz Well, why are they so famous? We all talk of the famous Marabar Caves. Perhaps that is our empty brag.

Godbole No, I should not quite say that.

Aziz Describe them to the lady, then.

Godbole It will be a great pleasure. (*Takes a mango.*) Mango season is almost over.

A long pause.

Aziz When I was a boy I used to run out to a big mango grove and gorge myself. My friends as well. Sometimes we would lie in the field, wet from the rain, our bodies covered with mango juice. We all ended up with painful stomachs. We have a proverb in Urdu – 'What does unhappiness matter when we are all unhappy together?'

He looks at **Adela**. **Adela**, *embarrassed, turns away.*

Adela I've never tasted a mango.

Godbole (*holds out a mango*) Please . . .

Adela *takes one.* **Ronny** *enters, followed by* **Fielding***'s* **Servant**. *He addresses* **Adela** *and does not acknowledge* **Aziz** *or* **Godbole**.

Ronny What's happened to Fielding? Where's my mother?

Adela (*coolly*) Good evening.

Ronny I want you and Mother at once. There's to be polo.

Godbole (*rises*) Your mother will return shortly, sir. There is but little to see at our poor college.

Ronny (*ignoring him*) I left work at an early hour because I thought the polo would give you pleasure.

Aziz Come along and join us, Mr Heaslop. Sit down till your mother shows up.

Ronny (*to* **Servant**) Please fetch your master at once.

Aziz Allow me. (*He repeats the phrase to the* **Servant** *in his native tongue.* **Ronny** *frowns.*) Ah – here they are at any rate.

Fielding *and* **Mrs Moore** *come in from the garden.*

Ronny Don't trouble to come in, Mother. We're just leaving.

Aziz *goes to* **Mrs Moore**. **Ronny** *takes* **Fielding** *aside.*

Ronny I say, old man, do excuse me, but I think you probably oughtn't to have left Miss Quested alone.

Fielding I'm sorry, what's up?

Ronny Well . . . I'm the sun-dried bureaucrat, no doubt, still I don't like to see an English girl left smoking with two Indians.

Fielding She stops, as she smokes, by her own wish, old man.

Ronny Yes, that's all right in England.

Fielding I really can't see the harm.

Ronny Can't you see that fellow's a bounder?

Fielding He isn't a bounder. His nerves seem a bit on edge, that's all.

Ronny What should have upset his precious nerves?

Fielding I don't know. He was all right when I left.

Ronny Well, it's nothing I said. I never even spoke to him.

Fielding Oh well, come along now, and take your ladies away; the catastrophe's over.

Ronny Fielding, don't think I'm taking it badly, or anything of that sort . . . I suppose you won't come on to the polo with us? We should all be delighted.

Fielding I'm afraid I can't, thanks all the same. I'm awfully sorry you feel I've been remiss. I didn't mean to be.

Mrs Moore Goodbye, Mr Fielding, and thank you so much . . . what lovely college buildings.

Fielding Goodbye, Mrs Moore.

Adela Goodbye, Mr Fielding. Such an interesting afternoon.

Fielding Goodbye, Miss Quested.

Mrs Moore Goodbye, Dr Aziz.

Aziz Goodbye, Mrs Moore.

Adela Goodbye, Dr Aziz.

Aziz Goodbye, Miss Quested. You'll jolly, jolly well not forget those caves, won't you? I'll fix the whole show up in a jiffy.

Adela Thank you.

Aziz What a shame you leave India so soon! Oh, do reconsider your decision. Do stay.

Ronny (*puzzled*) Adela?

Adela, *embarrassed, doesn't look at* **Ronny**: *she vigorously shakes* **Godbole**'s *hand.*

Adela Goodbye, Professor Godbole. It's a shame we never heard you sing.

Godbole I may sing now. (*Clears his throat.*)

Adela Oh.

Ronny Blast.

Godbole *sings. There is only an occasional illusion of a Western melody. The sound of his voice is hypnotic. It casts a spell over all except* **Ronny** *who, finally, bored and testy, walks into the garden.*

Adela *is transported by the music into another world. She is carried away by the sensuality of the music. She closes her eyes. She sees an image of two boys, almost naked, wet with rain and mango juice, wrestling in a field.*

She gasps. She is back in **Fielding**'s *room listening to* **Godbole** *sing.*

Godbole *stops halfway through a bar and sits down.*

Fielding Thanks so much; what was that?

Godbole I will explain in detail. It was a religious song. I placed myself in the position of a milk maiden. I say to Shri Krishna, 'Come! Come to me only.' The God refuses to come. I grow humble and say, 'Do not come to me only. Multiply yourself into a hundred Krishnas, and let one go to each of my hundred companions, but let one, O Lord of the Universe, one, come to me.' He refuses to come.

Mrs Moore But he comes in some other way, I hope.

Godbole Oh no. He refuses to come. I say to him, 'Come, come, come, come, come, come . . .' He neglects to come.

Mrs Moore Yes. I see. There is not enough God to go around.

Godbole *smiles.*

Riding in a tum-tum. **Mrs Moore** *sits in the front, next to a* **Driver**. **Ronny** *and* **Adela** *are in the back seat.*

Ronny What was that about caves?

Adela Mrs Moore, your doctor, whom I find delightful, has decided to invite us to a picnic out there – you, myself, Mr Fielding, Professor Godbole – exactly the same party.

Ronny Out where?

Adela The Marabar Caves.

Ronny Well I'm blessed. Did he descend to any details?

Adela He did not. If you had spoken to him, we could have arranged them. (**Ronny** *shakes his head, laughing.*) Have I said anything funny?

Ronny I was only thinking how your worthy doctor's collar climbed up his neck.

Adela I thought we were discussing the caves.

Ronny So I am. Aziz was exquisitely dressed, but he had forgotten his back collar stud, and there you have the Indians all over; inattention to detail.

Mrs Moore I like Aziz. Aziz is my real friend.

Ronny My point is they are unreliable. And naive. For instance, to 'meet' in the caves as if they were the clock at Charing Cross, when they're miles from a station and each other.

Adela Have you been to them?

Ronny No, but I know all about them, naturally.

Adela Oh, naturally!

Ronny Are you pledged to this expedition, Mother?

Mrs Moore Mother is pledged to nothing. Certainly not to this polo. I've never heard of these caves. I don't know what or where they are. But I really can't have so much quarrelling and tiresomeness. I want to be left off at the bungalow. Stop here.

The tum-tum stops. She stares at **Ronny** *and* **Adela**.

I feel increasingly that though people are important, the relations between them are not.

Ronny, *ashamed, helps her down. A* **Servant** *comes out to walk* **Mrs Moore** *back to the house.* **Ronny** *returns to the back seat.*

Ronny (*to* **Driver**) We'll go to the club now. (*The* **Driver** *doesn't respond.*) Damn. Not a word of English. Club. Club! (*The* **Driver** *starts again.*)

Adela We must have a thorough talk, Ronny, I'm afraid.

Ronny My temper's rotten, I must apologise. I didn't mean to order you and Mother about, but I know this Aziz will make some muddle over the caves.

Adela It's something very different, nothing to do with the caves, that I wanted to talk over with you. I've finally decided that we are not going to be married, dear boy.

Ronny (*pause – quietly*) You never said we should marry, my dear girl; you never bound either yourself or me – don't let this upset you.

Adela But let us discuss things; it's all so frightfully important, we mustn't make false steps. I want next to hear your point of view about me – it might help us both.

Ronny I don't much believe in this discussing.

Adela I only want everything to be absolutely clear between us and to answer any questions you care to put to me on my conduct.

Ronny But I haven't any questions. You've acted within your rights. You were quite right to come out and have a look at me doing my work, and anyhow, it's no use talking further – we should only get up steam.

Adela We've been awfully British over it, but I suppose that's all right.

Ronny As we are British, I suppose it is.

Adela Anyhow, we've not quarrelled, Ronny.

Ronny Oh, that would have been too absurd. Why should we quarrel?

Adela I think we shall keep friends.

Ronny I know we shall.

Adela Quite so.

Adela *fishes out a cigarette.*

Adela Let's not go to the club.

Ronny Shall I take you home?

Adela No. A drive. Fresh air.

Ronny (*to* **Driver**) No club. No club. (*Pantomimes.*) Drive. Country. Ganauati Road. No, no, sorry, it's under repair. Marabar Road.

Driver Ah. Marabar Road.

Adela Thank you. (*Pause.*) Oh. Listen . . .

Ronny What?

Adela To that bird. Did you hear it?

Ronny Yes.

Adela What do you think it was called?

Ronny I'm afraid I'm not good at birds; in fact, I'm useless at any information outside my own job.

Adela So am I. I'm useless at everything.

Ronny *and* **Adela** *sit stiffly next to each other, unable to converse any more.* **Godbole***'s song is heard in the faint distance.*

They hear the rustle of trees which seem to be calling to them: Come, come, come, come, come, come . . .

Aziz *appears in the front seat again, and turns and looks at* **Adela**. *He disappears. Darkness falls. The night is suddenly mysterious. A jolt.* **Adela***'s hand accidentally touches* **Ronny***'s. An intangible thrill seizes them. Neither withdraws their hand. They are surrounded by stars. But there are ominous shadows in the darkness.*

Suddenly – bump, jump, a swerve, the wheels lift in the air, brakes on, stand still. **Adela** *grips* **Ronny***'s hand, tightly.*

Ronny What's the damage?

The **Driver** *shouts in Urdu.*

Ronny Frightened, Adela?

Adela Not a bit.

Ronny Well, it's all over now. We skidded, I imagine.

Adela We didn't skid. We ran into an animal.

Ronny An animal?

Adela A large animal rushed up out of the dark on the right and hit us.

Ronny I didn't see an animal . . .

Pause; **Adela** *looks at him.*

. . . but, of course, if you say there was one, then, indeed there was one. (*Gets out and examines the right side of the car.*) Look, the paint's gone. It might have been a falling rock.

Adela I saw a hairy back quite plainly.

Ronny I say, Adela, what was it?

Adela I don't know the animals any better than the birds here – too big for a goat.

Ronny Let's look for its tracks.

Adela *and* **Ronny** *leave the car. The* **Driver** *hands them a torch.* **Ronny** *and* **Adela** *examine the ground near the car. They are a bit like children now.*

Ronny Do you think it was a buffalo?

Adela (*thrilled*) A buffalo? Perhaps.

Ronny (*searching for tracks*) Buffalo . . .

Adela Unless it was a hyena.

Ronny Hyena?

Adela (*smiles*) Yes, a hyena.

Ronny There aren't any tracks that are legible . . .

Another car approaches from the opposite side. **Ronny** *hails it.* **Miss Derek**, *a sporty young Englishwoman, sits inside.*

Ronny We've had a breakdown.

Miss Derek But how putrid!

Ronny We ran into a hyena.

Miss Derek How absolutely rotten.

Ronny Miss Derek. This is Miss Quested . . .

Adela Lovely to meet you.

Miss Derek What an adventure, eh?

Ronny Can you give us a lift?

Miss Derek Yes indeed . . .

Ronny *and* **Adela** *enter her car. They notice a dog asleep on the front seat. They sit in the back.* **Miss Derek** *starts her car again.*

She waves to the hapless **Driver**, *left stranded on the road as she speeds off.*

Miss Derek Cheerio! (*To* **Ronny** *and* **Adela**.) I've stolen the Maharaja's car. I'm companion to a maharanee, Miss Quested, in one of the Native States. She's an absolute dear, but he'll be very put out. (*Motions towards the dog.*) That's his fox terrier by the way. It's just that I needed a car for my holiday. I suppose he'll sack me, but if so, I'll get another job. The whole of India just seethes with maharanees and ronis and begums who clamour for such as me.

Ronny Really, I had no idea.

Miss Derek How could you have any idea, Mr Heaslop? What should he know about maharanees or the Hindu States.

Adela I understand those big people are not particularly interesting.

Adela *takes* **Ronny**'*s hand and squeezes it to signal her amusement at* **Miss Derek**. **Ronny** *smiles.*

Miss Derek Ah, there you are wrong. They're priceless. They're all quite eccentric, you know.

Adela *and* **Ronny** *laugh.* **Adela** *turns to* **Ronny** *nervously and says quietly:*

Adela Ronny, what I said earlier. . . you know. . .

Ronny Yes?

Adela I would like to take it back.

Ronny Oh, I'm so pleased. (*He smiles in relief, and squeezes her hand especially tight. Her other hand moves as if to touch him, but then modestly drops into her lap.*)

Mrs Moore, *in her room, writing a letter.*

Mrs Moore Dear Stella, dear Ralph, It seems my duties have finished now. Ronny is suited and after the wedding I shall return home. I don't want to see India now, not really.

I did so wish to say something enthusiastic – or encouraging – to Ronny and Adela about marriage, but I didn't know what. I rather feel that too much fuss is made over marriage; centuries of carnal embracement, yet man is no nearer to understanding man. Of course I said nothing of the sort. What is there to say – really – about anything? (*She pauses and then rips the letter in two.*)

Godbole*'s song is heard.*

Aziz *wakes up in bed sweating.* **Godbole***'s song fades away.*

Aziz *in bed.* **Hamidullah** *enters with* **Mahmoud Ali** *and* **Rafi**, *his nephew.*

Hamidullah Aziz, my dear fellow, we are greatly concerned.

Mahmoud Ali When a doctor falls ill, it is a serious matter.

The three men sit on **Aziz***'s bed.*

Rafi Dr Aziz took tea with our Mr Fielding last Thursday afternoon. Professor Godbole, who also attended, has sickened too, which seems a curious thing, does it not?

Aziz How do you do, young Rafi. How very kind of you to enquire after my health. How do you do, Hamidullah? But you bring me bad news. What is wrong with Godbole?

Hamidullah Why don't you answer, Rafi. You're the great authority.

Mahmoud Ali Yes, Rafi is the Sherlock Holmes of Chandrapore.

Rafi Diarrhoea.

Aziz If this is so, this is a very serious thing; diarrhoea before the end of March. Why have I not been informed?

Rafi Dr Panna Lal attends him, sir.

Aziz Oh yes, they are both Hindus; there we have it; they hang together like flies and keep everything dark. Rafi, tell me all the details. Is there vomiting also?

Rafi Oh yes, indeed, sir, and the stomach pains.

Aziz Alla! That settles it. In twenty-four hours he will be dead.

Mahmoud Ali All illness proceeds from Hindus.

Fielding *bursts into the room. The other visitors stand.*

Fielding I say, is he ill, or isn't he ill?

Aziz (*to the others*) Sit down.

Mahmoud Ali It is good of Mr Fielding to condescend to visit our friend. We are touched by this great kindness.

Aziz Don't talk to him like that, he doesn't want it.

Fielding Well, are you ill, Aziz, or aren't you?

Aziz We should be more concerned about Professor Godbole.

Fielding Oh yes. Poor chap evidently has haemorrhoids.

Aziz (*laughing, to* **Rafi**) Haemorrhoids – so much, my dear Sherlock, for your cholera.

Rafi But I never said the word cholera.

Hamidullah Dr Aziz is ill and he is not ill. And I suppose that most of us are in that same case. The whole world looks to be dying, still it doesn't die, so we must assume the existence of a beneficent Providence.

Fielding I'm afraid I don't believe in Providence.

Mahmoud Ali But how then can you believe in God?

Fielding I don't.

Hamidullah Is it correct that most are atheists in England now?

Fielding Actually, the West doesn't bother much about belief or disbelief in these days.

Hamidullah Excuse the question, but how is a country without real belief justified in holding India?

Fielding I'm out here personally because I needed a job. I cannot tell you why England is here or whether she ought to be here.

Hamidullah Then excuse me again – is it fair that Englishmen should occupy jobs when well-qualified Indians are available? Of course, I mean nothing personally. Personally we are delighted you should be here.

Fielding I'm delighted to be here too – that's my answer, that's my only excuse. I can't tell you anything about fairness.

Hamidullah And these Englishmen who are not delighted to be here – have they an excuse?

Fielding None. Chuck 'em out. (*They look at him amazed.*) Have I spoken out of turn?

Hamidullah You bewilder and amaze us, Mr Fielding. You are so frank. For us, what we say and what we feel are seldom the same.

Fielding Then you resemble your rulers, don't you think?

Aziz Rafi, Rafi!

Rafi Dr Aziz?

Aziz You sit on my leg.

Hamidullah Come along, we tire the invalid.

Mahmoud Ali Yes, we must conclude our visit.

Aziz Thank you, gentlemen. But Mr Fielding, may you linger a moment?

Fielding Certainly.

Hamidullah, **Mahmoud Ali** *and* **Rafi** *leave.*

Aziz Before you go, will you please unlock that drawer.

Fielding Where is the key?

Aziz Here. Round my neck. (*Points to a key that rests on a string around his neck.*) Please.

Fielding *is very hesitant; but then he removes the string from* **Aziz**'*s neck.*

Aziz The drawer. Please.

Fielding Are you certain?

Aziz Yes. Of course. What is the problem?

Fielding *goes to the drawer and opens it with the key.*

Aziz Do you see a piece of brown paper at the top?

Fielding Yes.

Aziz Open it.

Fielding (*removes a photograph*) Who is this?

Aziz She was my wife. You are the first Englishman she has ever come before. Now put her photograph away.

Fielding (*astonished, murmurs*) Really, I don't know why you pay me this great compliment, Aziz, but I do appreciate it.

Aziz You would have seen her, so why should you not see her photograph?

Fielding You would have allowed me to meet her?

Aziz Why not? All men are my brothers, and as soon as one behaves as such he may see my wife.

Fielding And when the whole world behaves as such, there will be no more purdah.

Aziz It is because you can say and feel such a remark as that, that I show you the photograph. Mr Fielding, no one can ever realise how much kindness we Indians need, we do not even realise it ourselves. But we know when it has been given. Kindness, more kindness, and even after that more kindness. I assure you it is the only hope. (*Pause.*) Put her away, she is of no importance, she is dead. I showed her to you because I have nothing else to show.

Fielding *puts the photograph away and sits on the bed. He returns the key to* **Aziz**. **Aziz** *motions to him to replace the key round his neck.* **Fielding** *does.*

Aziz Why are you not married?

Fielding Because I have more or less come through without it. (*Pause.*) The lady I liked wouldn't marry me – that is the main point, but that's fifteen years ago and now means nothing.

Aziz Why don't you marry Miss Quested?

Fielding Good God! Why, the girl's a prig. As it is, I can't marry her if I wanted to, for she has just become engaged to the City Magistrate.

Aziz Has she indeed? I am so glad. Of course, she is not beautiful. She has practically no breasts, if you come to think of it. I shall take you to Calcutta and arrange a lady with breasts like mangoes.

Fielding No you won't . . .

Aziz I suppose now she will be unable to attend the Marabar Caves?

Fielding I fear she is still expecting an invitation. I saw her yesterday on one of my rare visits to the club and she mentioned it.

Aziz Oh, I feel my fever returning. (*He falls back on to his pillows.*)

Godbole, *sitting on the carpet, addressing the audience.*

Godbole I miscalculated the length of a prayer. On that day. That particular day. For a moment I was ashamed of religion. Religion can, in a most literal way, make you miss the train. (*Pause.*) But the moment passed.

A train pulls into the Chandrapore station. Just before dawn. Smoke. Steam. Mist.

Aziz *is huddled in the station, with an ancient cousin of his,* **Mohammed Latif**, *and a group of* **Servants**.

Mrs Moore, **Adela** *and their Goanese servant,* **Anthony**, *walk out of the mist.* **Aziz** *rushes to meet them.*

Aziz But you've come after all. Oh, how very kind of you. This is the happiest moment of my life.

Mrs Moore We have so looked forward to this, Dr Aziz.

Adela We're so grateful that you've made the arrangements.

Aziz You come to the carriage and rest until Mr Fielding and the Professor can join us.

Servants *are running around with boxes, fruit, towels, a stepladder and a gun.* **Anthony** *watches everything, a smirk on his face.*

Aziz Send back your servant. He is unnecessary. Then we shall all be Moslems together.

Adela And he is such a horrible servant. Anthony, you can go. We don't want you.

Anthony Master told me to come.

Adela Mistress tells you to go.

Anthony Master says keep near the ladies all morning.

Adela Well, your ladies won't have you. Do get rid of him, Dr Aziz.

Aziz Mohammed Latif! Here is my cousin, Mr Mohammed Latif. Oh no, don't shake hands. He is an Indian of the old-fashioned sort, he prefers to salaam.

Mohammed Latif, how beautifully you salaam. See, he hasn't understood; he knows no English. Isn't he a funny old man? But you get inside now, make yourselves at home; yes, you must lie down. Excuse me now, I must meet our other two guests.

Aziz *looks at his watch.* **Mrs Moore** *and* **Adela** *enter their compartment on the train.*

Mohammed Latif *takes out some money and bribes* **Anthony** *who ultimately leaves the platform.*

Aziz, *meanwhile, paces up and down the platform. Suddenly he sees* **Fielding** *and* **Godbole** *at the level crossing, held up behind a barricade.*

Aziz Ah, there they are! Mr Fielding! Mr Fielding!

He shrieks from the pullman carriage. The train has started to move.

Merciful God!

Aziz *and* **Mohammed Latif** *fling themselves on to the train and leap on to the footground of a carriage.* **Mrs Moore** *and* **Adela** *are looking out of their compartment window.* **Aziz**, *holding on to a bar, shouts at them.*

Aziz We're monkeys, don't worry! (*Screams to* **Fielding** *again.*) Mr Fielding!

The level crossing bar lifts. **Fielding** *and* **Godbole** *rush forward. The train is about to pass them.*

Aziz (*shouts to* **Fielding**) Bad, bad, you have destroyed me.

Fielding Godbole's prayers did it.

Aziz Jump on, I must have you.

Fielding Right, give me a hand.

Mrs Moore He's not to, he'll kill himself.

Fielding *jumps, misses* **Aziz***'s hand and falls back on to the line. The train rumbles past.*

Aziz Mrs Moore, Miss Quested, our expedition is a ruin. (*Inches towards their compartment.*)

Mrs Moore Get in, get in, you'll kill yourself as well as Mr Fielding. I see no ruin.

Aziz How is that?

Mrs Moore We shall all be Moslems together, as you promised.

Aziz (*smiles*) Mrs Moore, I would die to make you happy.

Mrs Moore Oh, tosh. Just get in, Dr Aziz, you make us giddy.

Aziz *crawls into their compartment, followed by* **Mohammed Latif**.

Aziz Mohammed Latif, what is in these caves, brother? Why are we going to see them?

The train rides through the dawn. Then it slows alongside an elephant. It stops. A platform is placed leading from the ladies' carriage to the elephant.

Aziz It takes an hour to get there, an hour to get back, and two hours for the caves. Four hours – quite a small expedition – and an hour extra for misfortunes. If at any point you wish an alteration to the plans, you must tell me and it is done. Do you agree? Then mount this wild animal.

The elephant kneels. They come up a ladder and mount the elephant. The elephant rises and walks towards the hills. Below the elephant – sounds of villagers, babies, servants. A strange spiritual silence as the elephant moves forward. Then from the hills a brief whisper of **Godbole***'s song . . .*

Godbole Come, come, come, come . . .

The whisper fades away.

The elephant arrives at a place of stones and rocks and boulders.

Aziz Do you ever remember our mosque, Mrs Moore?

Mrs Moore I do, I do.

Aziz And how tough and rude I was and how good you were.

Mrs Moore And how happy we both were.

Aziz Friendships last longest that begin like that, I think. Shall I ever entertain your other children?

Adela Do you know about the others? She will never talk about them to me.

Aziz Ralph and Stella, yes, I know everything about them.

The elephant stops. **Adela** *and* **Mrs Moore** *are helped down.* **Adela** *suddenly shrieks.*

Mrs Moore What is it?

Adela (*points to the ground*) A snake!

Aziz Yes. It must be a black cobra. Very venomous.

Adela *takes out a pair of field glasses and looks through them.*

Adela No. No. It isn't a snake.

Aziz Isn't a snake?

Adela Just a tree stump, I think.

Aziz It's striking, isn't it?

Mrs Moore (*quietly, to* **Adela**) A horrid, stuffy place, I think.

A **Servant** *brings them tea.*

Mrs Moore How very well it is all arranged.

Adela You know, Dr Aziz, that I am going to marry Mrs Moore's son.

Aziz Ah, of course – Mr Heaslop. On which my heartfelt congratulations.

Adela Mrs Moore, may I put our difficulty to Dr Aziz – I mean our Anglo-Indian one?

Mrs Moore It is your difficulty, not mine, my dear.

Adela Ah, that's true. Well – by marrying Mr Heaslop I shall become what is known as Anglo-Indian.

Aziz Impossible. Take back such a terrible remark.

Adela But I shall, it's inevitable. I can't avoid the label. What I do hope to avoid is the mentality. Some of the women are so – well, ungenerous and snobby about Indians, and I should feel too ashamed for words if I turned like them, but there's nothing special about me, nothing specially good or strong, which will help me to resist my environment and avoid becoming like them. I've most lamentable defects.

Aziz You are absolutely unlike the others, I assure you. You will never be rude to my people.

Adela I am told we all get rude after a year.

Aziz Then you are told a lie.

Mrs Moore *closes her eyes.*

Aziz Come – let us explore the caves.

Mrs Moore *opens her eyes.*

Mrs Moore Pardon?

Aziz The caves . . .

Mrs Moore Oh, but surely we can't all go in. We are such a crowd.

Aziz Just villagers. Very friendly.

Mrs Moore And the animals?

Aziz Oh yes. And the babies as well. They are all very proud of their caves.

Mrs Moore *smiles but is obviously reluctant to move.*

They move into the cave.

Godbole *sitting on the carpet, addressing the audience.*

Godbole It is not possible. I will not even try to describe the caves. They are dark, of course. Even when they open towards the sun, very little light penetrates down the entrance tunnel into the circular chamber. There is little to see, and no eye to see it, until the visitor arrives for his five minutes and strikes a match.

Mrs Moore*'s face: she has entered a cave.*

Adela *and* **Aziz** *are there as well. Villagers, babies, animals, servants also. It's as if all of India were in this one small cave. Indeed, it is as if the cave were made out of the people. The cave is dark. We can only see* **Mrs Moore**. *Everything, everyone else is in shadow.* **Mrs Moore** *is breathless. She feels faint.*

Godbole*'s song insinuates itself in the distance, then disappears when* **Aziz** *lights a match, which produces an echo.* **Mrs Moore** *holds her ears. Some naked thing strikes her face. A baby's hand, but she cannot see it. She tries to return to the entrance, but the influx of villagers sweeps her back. She hits her head. For an instance, she goes mad, hitting and gasping like a fanatic. The echo continues. It is devoid of distinction – boom is the sound – but it is terrifying.* **Mrs Moore** *is overwhelmed by sound and smells and humanity; the cave seems to be moving in circles. She is swept back to the entrance. She rushes out of the cave into the sunlight.*

Mrs Moore *stands outside the cave, gasping. She looks at the others emerging and realises that none are villains.*

Adela *is now standing by her.*

Adela Did you see the reflection of his match? Rather pretty.

Mrs Moore I forgot.

Adela But he says this isn't a good cave, the best are on the other side.

Mrs Moore I don't think I shall go on to there.

Adela Very well, let's sit down again in the shade until breakfast is ready.

Mrs Moore Ah, but that'll disappoint him; he has taken so much trouble. You should go on; I don't mind.

Adela Perhaps I ought to.

Aziz *comes to them.*

Adela Mrs Moore wishes to rest a while. She would like us to go ahead without her.

Aziz Certainly, Miss Quested, then you and I will go together.

Mrs Moore Quite right. I'm sorry not to come too but I am a poor walker.

Aziz Dear Mrs Moore, what does anything matter so long as you are my guest. I am very glad that you are not coming, which sounds strange, but you are treating me with true frankness, as a friend.

Mrs Moore (*lays her hand on his sleeve tenderly*) Yes. I am your friend. (*Pause.*) So may I make another suggestion? Don't let so many people with you this time. I think you may find it more convenient.

Aziz Exactly, exactly. (*To* **Servants**.) We will only take one guide with us.

Mrs Moore Quite right. Now, enjoy yourselves, and when you come back, tell me all about it.

She sinks into a deckchair. **Aziz, Adela** *and a* **Guide** *start off.* **Mrs Moore** *takes out a writing pad and starts to write.*

Mrs Moore Dear Stella, dear Ralph. (*She stops. She looks over at* **Mohammed Latif**.) Did you hear that noise in the cave? There was a sound. Do you understand me? No? Good. Something spoke to me, something very old and very small, something before time, before space also. Did you hear it? Something incapable of generosity. Do you feel despair? Perhaps the despair I feel is only *my* despair, my own personal weakness. After all, if I suddenly got sunstroke and went mad the rest of the world would go on, wouldn't it? (*He smiles at her, uncomprehending.*) I don't want to write to my children. I don't want to commmunicate with anyone, not even God. (*Her words frighten her. She sits motionless with terror.*)

Aziz, Adela *and the* **Guide** *climb rocks leading to the larger caves.*

Aziz I'm sure we'll find some interesting carvings in the next caves.

Adela Oh yes. I would think so.

Aziz *and* **Adela** *voice their inner thoughts, interspersed with their public conversation.*

Aziz (*inner thoughts*) I have very little to say to this woman. I do not like her near as much as Mrs Moore.

Aziz You're not too hot?

Adela No. I'm fine. Thank you.

Adela (*inner thoughts*) I must stop complaining about Anglo-Indians. There is still so much to do. I know there will be difficulties – Ronny's limitations and my own – but I enjoy facing difficulties. I think our married life can be happy and profitable. I mustn't be too theoretical; I'll deal with each problem as it comes up; I'll trust in Ronny's common sense and my own. Luckily we both have an abundance of common sense. (*Pause.*) But what about love? Ronny and I do not love each other.

Aziz Would you like to rest?

Adela No, please let's go on. (*Inner thoughts.*) Ronny and I do not love each other.

Aziz It gets steep here. Take my hand.

Adela Thank you. (*She takes his hand.*)

Aziz Did I take you too fast?

Adela (*inner thoughts*) Not to love the man one's going to marry! Not to find it out until this moment! Not even to have asked oneself the question until now! (*Public.*) No, I'm all right, thanks. (*Inner thoughts.*) Should I break the engagement? It would cause so much trouble to others. Besides, I'm not convinced that love is necessary to a successful union. (*Public.*) Are you married, Dr Aziz?

Aziz Yes indeed.

Adela And have you children?

Aziz Yes indeed. Three.

Adela And they are a great pleasure to you?

Aziz Why, naturally I adore them. (*Inner thoughts.*) I suppose her breasts are sufficient for the City Magistrate.

Adela (*inner thoughts*) What a handsome little Oriental he is.

Aziz (*inner thoughts*) But her face is so plain.

Adela (*inner thoughts*) I suppose he must attract women of his own race.

Aziz (*inner thoughts*) She has no physical charm.

Adela (*inner thoughts*) I have no physical charm. It does make a difference in a relationship – beauty, thick hair, a fine skin. (*Public.*) Have you one wife or more than one?

Aziz (*inner thoughts*) How can she ask that! I am an educated Moslem. How can she ask . . . (*Public.*) One, one in my particular case. (*Lets go of her hand. Inner thoughts.*) Damn the English, even at their best!

Adela We have arrived.

Aziz Yes. We have. One moment, if you please . . .

Aziz *walks off and disappears round a bend.* **Adela** *looks ahead of her to the entrance of the caves and then back at the rocks.*

It is suddenly very hot. She wipes her brow. She hears **Godbole***'s song in the distance:* 'Come, come, come, come . . .' *She moves towards the entrance of the cave, and then, in a split second, unseen by the* **Guide***, walks into it.*

She is alone in the cave, enveloped by darkness. She lights a match.

A terrifying echo: BOOM!!!!!!!!!!!!

Darkness.

Aziz *sits inside another cave, smoking. He composes himself. He leaves and returns to the rocks where he left* **Adela***. Only the* **Guide** *is there, listening to a noise below.*

Aziz What is that?

Guide Noise.

Aziz It sounds like a motor car. (*Looks down over the rocks.*) Yes, coming towards the hills. Let's tell Miss Quested. (*Pause.*) Where is she?

Guide She goes into the cave.

Aziz Which cave?

Guide One of those.

Aziz What? You should have kept her in sight, it was your duty. Here are twelve caves at least. How am I to know which one contains my guest? Which even is the cave I was in myself? (*Looks at caves and is even unsure which direction he came from.*) Merciful heavens, Miss Quested is lost. Shout. Shout her name. Miss Quested!

Guide Miss Quested!

Aziz Miss Quested!

Her name echoes through the rocks. **Aziz** *is sweating. He wipes his head. He goes into one cave. Then another. Nothing.*

Come here. (*The* **Guide** *goes to him.*) This is the end of my career, my guest is lost.

Aziz *strikes the* **Guide** *in the face. He starts back towards the rocks, then notices something on the ground. He bends down and picks up* **Adela***'s field glasses.*

Aziz Oh my God! Her field glasses!

The loud scream of a train whistle! Smoke. Noise.

The train platform at Chandrapore.

Aziz, Mohammed Latif *and* **Mrs Moore** *enter onto the platform.* **Fielding** *rushes up to meet them.*

Fielding I'm so sorry we missed the train. Godbole's prayers took longer than expected. Where is Miss Quested?

Aziz She went for a spin.

Ronny *pushes through the crowd, followed by* **Mr Haq**, *a police officer.*

Mrs Moore Ronny!

Ronny Come away now, Mother. (*Takes her arm.*)

Mrs Moore Dr Aziz, I must thank you . . .

Ronny Instantly, Mother! I insist! (*He forcefully pulls a protesting* **Mrs Moore** *away.* **Mr Haq** *steps forward.*)

Haq Dr Aziz, it is my highly painful duty to arrest you.

Fielding Hello, some mistake.

Haq They are my instructions.

Fielding This is nonsense. On what charge do you arrest him?

Haq I am under instructions not to say. Refer to Inspector McBryde.

Fielding Very well. Come along, Aziz, old man; nothing to fuss about, some blunder.

Aziz *sobs. He suddenly tries to bolt.* **Fielding** *pulls him back.*

Fielding Oh, for God's sake . . . Never, never act a criminal.

Aziz (*softly*) My children and my name.

Fielding Nothing of the sort. Put your hat straight and take my arm. I'll see you through.

Aziz *takes* **Fielding**'*s arm. They are escorted by* **Mr Haq** *who is joined by other* **Policemen**. **Mohammed Latif** *starts to wail. Suddenly* **Haq** *and another* **Policeman** *pry* **Aziz** *away from* **Fielding**.

Aziz Fielding – don't leave me.

The platform is a madhouse. Passengers and porters in all directions. Steam. The **Policemen** *carrying* **Aziz** *away.*

A train whistle blares, and it merges with a woman's scream. **Adela**. *She is on one side of the stage, hysterical.* **Miss Derek** *is attending her, mopping her brow and painfully picking cactus needles out of her arms and legs.*

The echo is heard: BOOM!!!!!

On the other side of the stage – **Fielding** *and* **McBryde**, *the Superintendent of Police, in the Police Station.*

McBryde All natives are criminals at heart, for the simple reason that they live south of latitude 30. They are not to blame, they have not a dog's chance – we should be like them if we settled here.

Fielding For God's sake, McBryde, what on earth has happened?

McBryde I'm afraid Miss Quested has been insulted in one of the Marabar Caves.

Fielding Oh no, oh no, no, no.

McBryde She escaped by God's grace. Although she is poorly.

Fielding Oh no, no, but not Aziz . . . not Aziz . . . (**McBryde** *nods.*) What is the charge, precisely?

McBryde That he followed her into the cave and made insulting advances. She hit at him with her field glasses, he pulled at them and the strap broke, and that is how she got away. When we searched him just now they were in his pocket. I couldn't worry her overmuch with questions. She is in a shocking state. There was an echo that appears to have frightened her. Major Callender is very concerned about her health. Her entire body has been punctured by cactus needles. Utterly barbaric. I heard some more from Miss Derek. She heard stones falling and saw Miss Quested running straight down the face of a precipice. Well. She climbed up a sort of gully to her and found her practically done for. She had got among the cactuses. Miss Derek saved her life coming just then . . .

Fielding I believe Miss Quested must be under some hideous delusion and that the wretched boy is innocent.

McBryde I had no idea that was in your mind.

Fielding Those field glasses upset me for a minute, but I've thought since: it's impossible that, having attempted to assault her, he would put her glasses into his pocket.

McBryde Quite possible, I'm afraid; when an Indian goes bad, he goes not only very bad, but very queer. The Lord help us, the Lord help us all.

Major Callender *gives* **Adela** *an injection, as* **Miss Derek** *watches.*

Fielding *and* **Godbole** *at* **Fielding***'s house.*

Godbole Ah, Mr Fielding, I am pleased to find you. I have an interesting proposition for you to ponder.

Fielding I see the news has not reached you yet.

Godbole Oh yes.

Fielding No: there has been a terrible catastrophe about Aziz.

Godbole Oh yes. That is all round the college.

Fielding I am most frightfully cut up.

Godbole So I saw at once on entering your office. I must not detain you, but I have a small private difficulty on which I want your help: I am leaving your service shortly as you know. And am returning to my birthplace, Mau, in Central India. I want to start a high school there on sound English lines, but the point on which I desire your help is this – what name should be given to the school?

Fielding (*feeling slightly ill*) A name? A name for a school?

Godbole Yes, a name, a suitable title, by which it can be called.

Fielding Really – I have no names for schools in my head. I can think of nothing but poor Aziz. Have you grasped that at the present moment he is in prison?

Godbole Oh yes. Oh no, I do not expect an answer to my question now. I had thought of the Mr Fielding High School, but failing that King Emperor the Fifth.

Fielding Godbole! (**Godbole** *puts his hands together.*) Is Aziz innocent or guilty?

Godbole That is for the court to decide. The verdict will be in strict accordance with the evidence. I make no doubt.

Fielding Yes, yes, but your personal opinion. Would he or would he not do such a thing?

Godbole Ah. A complicated question. (*Pause.*) The tragedy, of course, is that you missed the interesting Marabar antiquities.

Fielding *groans.*

Adela *sits up in bed now, staring vacantly into space. She remains there for the rest of the act.*

Fielding *walks through the bazaar. A tiger jumps out of the darkness. But it is only a youth dressed up as a tiger, the body striped brown and yellow, a mask over his face. The Festival of Mohurram is beginning. There are drummers on all sides. The drumming is good-natured.* **Fielding** *continues on his way.*

The club. Drumming is heard in the distance. **Turton** *addresses* **Mrs Turton** *and a group of* **Englishwomen**. *A young* **Subaltern** *is also present, as well as several other club members, including* **Mr Burton**.

Turton Not the least cause for alarm. Keep cool, keep cool. Don't go out more than you can help, don't go into the city, don't talk before your servants. That's all.

Mrs Turton Harry, is there any news from the city?

Turton Everything absolutely normal.

Mrs Turton Mr McBryde's down there disguised as a Holy Man.

Turton That's exactly the sort of thing that must not be said, Mary, be more careful than that, please. We must not say anything that will cause alarm . . . Are there any questions?

Englishwoman (Mrs Blakiston) What if the niggers attack?

Turton They won't, Mrs Blakiston, and anyhow, they're not coming to the club.

Mrs Turton But those drums . . .

Turton Merely Mohurram. Some kind of festival. No need to worry. We have everything well in hand. Will all the ladies leave the smoking room now, please? And remember what I have said. You can help us by behaving as if everything is normal. Can I rely on you?

Ladies Yes indeed . . . Oh indeed . . .

The **Ladies** *leave.* **Fielding** *had slipped into the room during their talk. The* **Subaltern** *glares at him.*

Turton Don't go carrying arms about. I want everything to proceed as usual, until there's cause for the contrary. Get the womenfolk off to the hills, but do it quietly.

Subaltern Exactly what I said.

Burton This nonsense would never have happened if we were under military control.

Turton (*stares at him, coldly*) Soldiers put one thing straight, but leave a dozen others crooked.

Major Callender *enters.*

Turton Major Callender, how is your patient?

Callender No one's out of danger in this country as long as they have a temperature.

Turton How's the old lady?

Callender Temperature.

Turton My wife heard she was sinking.

Callender I guarantee nothing. I really can't be plagued with questions. I wish to God I hadn't given my assistant leave. I'd cut my tongue out first. To feel I'm responsible; that's what hits me.

Turton No one blames you, my dear Callender.

Callender Heaslop found out something from his mother. Aziz paid a herd of natives to suffocate her in a cave. That was the end of her, or would have been, only she got out. Nicely planned, wasn't it? Then he could go with the girl. He and she and a guide, only the guide now can't be found. Pretty. It's time for action. Call in the troops and clear the bazaars.

Turton *clears his throat, makes a hand motion to calm things down.* **Ronny** *enters, looking exhausted and tragic. The others, in instinctive homage, rise to their feet.* **Fielding** *remains seated.*

Ronny Oh please, please, all sit down. I only wanted to listen to what has been decided.

Turton Heaslop, I'm telling them I'm against any show of force. When the verdict is obtained, it will be another matter.

Ronny You are sure to know best.

Turton How is your mother, old boy?

Ronny Better, thank you. I wish everyone would sit down.

Subaltern Some have never got up.

Turton Mr Fielding, what has prevented you from standing up?

Fielding May I make a statement, sir?

Turton Certainly.

Fielding (*rises*) I believe Dr Aziz to be innocent.

Turton You have a right to hold that opinion if you choose, but is that any reason why you should insult Mr Heaslop?

Fielding May I conclude my statement?

Turton Certainly.

Fielding I am waiting for the court. If he is guilty I resign from my service and leave India. I resign from the club.

Members Hear, hear.

Turton You have not answered my question. Why did you not stand when Mr Heaslop entered?

Fielding With all deference, sir, I am not here to answer questions but to make a personal statement and I have concluded it.

Turton One moment, Mr Fielding. You are not to go yet, please. Before you leave the club, from which you do very well to resign, will you express some detestation of the crime and will you apologise to Mr Heaslop?

Fielding Are you speaking to me officially, sir?

Turton (*infuriated*) Leave this room at once. You have sunk to the level of your associates.

Fielding *tries to reach the door but the* **Subaltern** *stands in his path, blocking him.*

Fielding I want to leave the room but cannot while this gentleman prevents me.

Ronny Let him go.

The **Subaltern** *moves aside reluctantly.* **Fielding** *walks out.*

Turton I'm afraid Mr Fielding has long been a disruptive force. If you remember he remarked last year that the white races are in fact really pinko-grey. Mrs Turton picked up on that at once. I tried to give the fellow a chance. After all, I don't believe in rushing to judgement.

Adela*'s eyes open wide. She starts to sit up, then falls back on the bed.*

Aziz *is in a prison cell. A* **Guard** *opens the door.* **Fielding** *walks in.*

Aziz Cyril, why did you desert me?

Fielding I did not desert you.

Aziz I thought you would not come.

Fielding I am here now. I am here.

They reach out to each other – and grasp their hands together.

Godbole *enters.*

Godbole Tonight when our ceremony begins and our God is born, infinite love will take the form of Shri Krishna and save the world. All sorrow will disappear, not only for Indians, but for foreigners, birds, caves, railways and the stars. All will become joy and laughter, there will have been no disease, no doubt, misunderstanding, cruelty, fear. It happens in a moment, and then . . . once we have thought we were with God, that moment becomes history and disappears.

Act Two

Mau. **Professor Godbole**, *barefoot and in white, addresses the audience.*

Godbole You ask about the Marabar Caves. You ask what happened. You ask about the 'mystery'. What you want to know is: did our friend Dr Aziz commit an evil action. Assuming an action, any action, was committed. Would you like me to answer? Ah, but the question is a difficult one in our philosophy. It presumes that an individual can commit good actions or evil actions. Difficult. Because nothing can be performed in isolation. All perform a good action, when one is performed, and when an evil action is performed, all perform it. To illustrate my meaning let me take the case in point as an example. My answer is this: if such an action was performed, it was performed by Dr Aziz. (*Pause.*) It was performed by the guide. (*Pause.*) It was performed by me. It was performed by you. And by my students. It was even performed by the lady herself. Does that solve the 'mystery' for you? You see, when evil occurs, it expresses the whole of the universe. Similarly when good occurs. Good and evil are not what we think them, they are both what they are, and each of us has contributed to them both. Perhaps you ask then are good and evil the same? Oh no, you must not think that. Good and evil are different, as their names imply. But in my own humble opinion they are both of them aspects of my Lord. He is present in the one, absent in the other, and the difference between presence and absence is great. Yet absence implies presence, absence is not nonexistence, and we are therefore entitled to repeat 'Come, come, come, come . . .' (*Pause.*) I hope that answers your questions. Now the holy festival is to begin. Our God is soon to be born. And the Sweepers Band will soon arrive. Our God, once born, cannot leave his temple until the unclean sweepers play their tune. It takes a spot of filth, after all, for the spirit to cohere.

The mist returns and Mau disappears.

Chandrapore. **Aziz** *walks through the mist.* **Indians** *surround him, shouting. They begin to riot. They throw rocks, break windows.* **Aziz** *is swallowed up by the crowd.*

Adela *sits in a chair – on the other side of the stage. She is dressed.* **Miss Derek** *attends her. Noises of the rioting can be heard outside.*

Adela I went into this detestable cave . . .

Miss Derek There's no need to go through it again . . .

Adela And I remember scratching the wall with my fingernail . . .

On the other side of the stage – a prison cell. **Fielding** *visiting* **Aziz**.

Aziz Two hours!

Fielding You were free for two hours?

Aziz Yes. On bail. But as soon as they released me the riots started. So they returned me to prison and honoured me with an additonal charge: disturbing the public peace.

Fielding I brought you some mangoes.

Adela *is continuing her tale.*

Adela . . . and then as I was saying there was this shadow, or sort of shadow, down the entrance tunnel, bottling me up. It seemed like an age, but I suppose the whole thing can't have lasted thirty seconds really. I hit at him with the glasses, he pulled me round the cave by the strap, it broke, I escaped, that's all. He never actually touched me once. It all seems such nonsense.

Miss Derek My dear . . .

Adela You've been so kind to me. How can I ever repay you? How can one repay when one has nothing to give? I'm not fit for personal relationships – of any kind.

Miss Derek (*touches her arm*) My dear . . .

Adela No, no, don't touch me – please.

The prison cell.

Aziz Do you know who my favourite emperor is? Not Alamgir, as you might imagine. No, it is Babar. Not a pious man, like Alamgir. And you know how he died? He laid down his life for his son. They were caught in the desert heat. His son fell sick. Babar walked round his son's bed three times and said, 'I have borne it away,' and he did bear it away; the fever left his son and came to him instead, and he died. This is why I prefer Babar to Alamgir. (*He takes the mangoes from* **Fielding**.)

Ronny*'s bungalow.* **Mrs Moore** *sits on a sofa, looking at a list of steamship sailings.* **Ronny** *enters with a very fragile* **Adela**. **Mrs Moore** *does not get up.*

Mrs Moore Here you are both back.

Adela *sits down and takes* **Mrs Moore***'s hand.* **Mrs Moore** *withdraws it.*

Ronny Are you all right? You appeared all right when I left.

Mrs Moore I am all right. As a matter of fact I have been looking at my return ticket. It is interchangeable so I have a much larger choice of boats home than I thought.

Ronny We can go into that later, can't we?

Mrs Moore Ralph and Stella may be wanting to know when I arrive.

Ronny There is plenty of time for all such plans. How do you think our Adela looks?

Adela (*to* **Mrs Moore**) I am counting on you to help me through; it is such a blessing to be with you again. These past two weeks at the McBrydes were very difficult; I was, of course – well – feverish for some of the time and they were all so kind, but still, they were strangers. I know it's all nothing; I must be sensible, I do try – but there is this echo that I keep on hearing.

Mrs Moore Oh, what of the echo?

Adela I can't get rid of it.

Mrs Moore I don't suppose you ever will.

Adela Mrs Moore, what is this echo?

Mrs Moore Don't you know?

Adela No, what is it? Oh, do say! I felt you would be able to explain it.

Mrs Moore If you don't know, you don't know; I can't tell you.

Adela I think you're rather unkind not to say.

Mrs Moore Say, say, say. As if anything can be said! I have spent my life in saying or in listening to sayings! I have listened too much. It is time I was left in peace. Not to die. No doubt you expect me to die, but when I have seen you and Ronny married and seen the other two and whether they want to be married – I'll retire into a cave of my own. (*Smiles.*) Somewhere where no young people will come asking questions and expecting answers. Some shelf.

Ronny Quite so, but meantime a trial is coming up. (*To* **Adela**.) The case will come before Das, my assistant. He's intelligent and of course can only come to one conclusion. Still, the notion of most of us is that we'd better pull together and help one another through, instead of . . . (*Looks at* **Mrs Moore**.) being disagreeable. Are you going to talk like that in the witness box?

Mrs Moore Why should I be in the witness box?

Ronny To confirm certain points in our evidence.

Mrs Moore I have nothing to do with your ludicrous law courts. I will not be dragged in at all.

Adela I won't have her dragged in either. I won't have any more trouble on my account. (*Takes* **Mrs Moore**'s *hand, which is again withdrawn.*) Her evidence is not the least essential.

Ronny I thought she would want to give it. No one blames you, Mother, but the fact remains that you dropped off at the first cave, and encouraged Adela to go on with him alone, whereas if you'd been well enough to keep on too, nothing would have happened. Forgive me for speaking so plainly but you've no right to take up this high and mighty attitude about law courts. I thought you would want to take your part; I really did.

Mrs Moore I shall attend your marriage, but not your trial. Then I shall go to England.

Ronny You can't go to England in May. We agreed.

Mrs Moore I have changed my mind.

Ronny You appear to want to be left out of everything.

Mrs Moore My body, my miserable body. Why isn't it strong? Oh, why can't I walk away and be gone? Why can't I finish my duties and be gone? Why do I get headaches and puff when I walk? And all the time this to do in her way and that to do in your way, and everything sympathy and confusion and bearing one another's burdens. Why can't this be done and that be done in my way and they be done and I at peace? Why has anything to be done, I cannot see. Why all this marriage, marriage? . . . The human race would have become a single person centuries ago if marriage was any use. And all this rubbish about love, love in a church, love in a cave, as if there is the least difference, and I held up from my business over such trifles!

Ronny What do you want? Can you state it in simple language? If so, do.

Mrs Moore I want my pack of patience cards.

Ronny Very well, get them.

Mrs Moore *rises and walks out of the room.* **Adela** *starts to weep.*

Ronny Well, my dear girl, this isn't much of a homecoming. I had no idea she had this up her sleeve.

Adela *stops crying. She looks both relieved and horrified.*

Adela Aziz, Aziz . . .

Ronny What the dickens? . . .

Adela Aziz . . . have I made a mistake?

Ronny You're overtired.

Adela Ronny, he's innocent; I made an awful mistake.

Ronny Sit down . . . please . . .

They sit. She takes his hand and strokes it and smiles, then gasps and touches her ear.

Adela My echo's better.

Ronny That's good. You'll be perfectly well in a few days, but you must save yourself up for the trial.

Adela But Ronny, Ronny dear, perhaps there oughtn't to be any trial.

Ronny I don't quite know what you're saying, and I don't think you do.

Adela If Dr Aziz never did it he ought to be let out. (*Clings to him.*) Help me to do what I ought. Aziz is good. You heard your mother say so.

Ronny Heard what?

Adela He's good; I've been so wrong to accuse him.

Ronny Mother never said so.

Adela Didn't she?

Ronny She never mentioned the name once.

Adela But Ronny, I heard her.

Ronny Pure illusion. You can't be quite well, can you, to make up a thing like that?

Adela I suppose I can't. How amazing of me.

Ronny I was listening to all she said, as far as it could be listened to: she gets very incoherent.

Adela When her voice dropped she said it – towards the end, when she talked about love – love – I couldn't follow, but just then she said, 'Dr Aziz never did it.'

Ronny Those words?

Adela The idea more than the words.

Ronny Never, never, my dear girl. His name was not mentioned by anyone. So you won't go on saying he's innocent again, will you? For every servant I've got is a spy.

Mrs Moore *returns with her patience cards and sits at the card table.*

Ronny Mother, did you mention the prisoner's name?

Mrs Moore I don't understand the question.

Ronny Adela thought she heard you say the prisoner's name.

Mrs Moore I never said his name. (*Begins to play patience.*)

Adela I thought you said, 'Aziz is an innocent man.'

Mrs Moore Of course he is innocent.

Adela You see, Ronny, I was right.

Ronny You were not right, she never said it.

Adela But she thinks it.

Ronny Who cares what she thinks.

Mrs Moore (*from the card table*) Red nine on black ten.

Ronny She can think whatever she wants, but there's such a thing as evidence, I suppose.

Adela I know, but –

Mrs Moore Is it again my duty to talk? Apparently, as you keep interrupting me.

Ronny Only if you have anything sensible to say.

Mrs Moore Oh, why is everything still my duty? When shall I be free from your fuss? Was he in the cave and were you in the cave and on and on. . . and unto us a son is born, unto us a child is given . . . and am I glad and is he bad and are we saved? . . . and ending everything, the echo.

Adela I don't hear it so much. You send it away, you do nothing but good, you are good.

Mrs Moore I am not good, no, bad. (*Returns to her cards.*) A bad old woman, bad, bad, detestable. I used to be good with the children growing up. Also I met the young man in his mosque, I wanted him to be happy. Good, happy, small people. They don't exist, they were a dream. But I will not help you to torture him for what he never did. Nothing happened, and if it had, there are worse evils than love.

Ronny Have you any evidence in the prisoner's favour? If so, it is your bounded duty to go into the witness box for him instead of for us. No one will stop you.

Mrs Moore One knows people's characters, as you call them. I feel it isn't the sort of thing he would do.

Ronny Feeble, Mother, feeble.

Mrs Moore Most feeble.

Ronny And most inconsiderate to Adela.

Adela It would be so appalling if I was wrong. I should take my own life.

Ronny What was I warning you just now? You know you're right, and the whole station knows it.

Adela Yes, he . . . This is very very awful. I'm as certain as ever he followed me . . . only wouldn't it be possible to withdraw the case? I dread the idea of giving evidence more and more . . . Oh, of course, it's out of the question, I'm ashamed to have mentioned it; please forgive me.

Ronny That's all right. The case has to come before a magistrate now; it really must, the machinery has started.

Mrs Moore She has started the machinery; it will work to its end.

Ronny (*stares at her*) Perhaps you're right, Mother. Perhaps you should leave India at once. (*He picks up the list of steamship sailings.*)

A prison cell. **Aziz** *is with* **Fielding**, **Hamidullah** *and* **Rafi**.

Rafi The sweepers are on strike, and remain so until you are acquitted.

Hamidullah A number of Mohammedan Indians have sworn to take no food until you are acquitted.

Aziz Their death will make little difference.

Fielding Why do you say so, my friend?

Aziz Because it has been decided already. Has it not? It is fate!

The others look at him and cannot speak.

A **Young Man**, *almost naked, sits on a raised platform and pulls a punkah – a large fixed and swinging fan, formed of cloth, stretched on a rectangular frame, suspended from the ceiling.*

It is the courtroom.

The asssistant magistrate, **Das**, *cultivated, self-conscious and conscientious, sits on a platform in the centre.* **Ronny**, **Adela**, **Mrs Turton** *and* **Major Callender** *enter on one side. They are joined by* **McBryde** *who will be prosecuting. On the other side, a pale and nervous* **Aziz**, *flanked by his legal team,* **Mahmoud Ali** *and a fine-looking barrister from Calcutta,* **Amritrao**. **Fielding** *enters the courtroom. There is a frisson as he takes a seat next to the Indians. He does not look at the British.*

Adela *and* **Aziz** *turn and stare at each other. Suddenly* **Godbole**'*s song is heard and everyone fades from view, except for* **Adela** *and* **Aziz**, *who are both pinpointed in isolated lights. They can only see each other. They are surrounded by shadows – shadows of their friends, shadows of the courtroom – and sound – the sound of the punkah and fluttering fans in the hands of the female spectators. The sounds of people gossiping and coughing. And the sound of the echo in* **Adela**'*s head. People try to crowd into their light, but we only see the outer edges of bodies. Voices merge into one another.*

Das Order, order . . .

Ronny I've given Das good training; he'll be all right. . .

Mrs Turton Not one of them's all right.

Ronny Das is, really.

Hamidullah We are lucky. Mr Amritrao is a Calcutta barrister with a high professional reputation.

Fielding And notoriously anti-British. Aziz must be cleared with the minimum of racial hatred.

Hamidullah Oh no, we must hit with all our strength.

Fielding We're bound to win. She will never be able to substantiate the charge.

Mrs Turton You mean your Das is more frightened of acquitting than convicting because if he acquits he will lose his job.

Ronny Conviction is inevitable; so better let an Indian pronounce it.

Das Order! Superintendent McBryde, you may begin.

McBryde'*s shadow looms over* **Aziz**.

McBryde This man before us, this Dr Aziz, is guilty of a most heinous crime. Everyone knows this to be true, and I am obliged to say so in public. The darker races are physically attracted by the fairer, but not vice versa – not a matter of bitterness this, not a matter for abuse, but just a fact which any scientific observer will confirm.

Voice Even when the lady is uglier than the gentleman?

Das Turn that man out! If there are any other comments I will clear the gallery.

Mrs Turton Do you feel faint, Miss Quested?

Adela I never feel anything else.

Major Callender Really, old man, better arrangements should be made for Miss Quested. She gets no air. Why isn't she given a seat on the platform?

Das I shall be happy to accommodate Miss Quested with a chair up here in view of the particular circumstances of her health.

The bustle of chairs raised on to the platform. **Adela**, *pinpointed in her light, moves on to the platform; pieces of chairs are thrust into her light. We can sense that the entire British party has followed* **Adela** *on to the platform.*

Mrs Turton That's better.

Major Callender Right, McBryde, go ahead now; sorry to have interrupted you.

McBryde We will also show that the prisoner is a man of loose life, as photographs found upon him at his arrest will testify . . .

Mahmoud Ali May I ask why my client cannot be accommodated on the platform too; even Indians feel unwell sometimes.

Das Mr Mahmoud Ali, please take your seat. Mr Amritrao?

Amritrao Excuse me. We object to the presence of so many European ladies and gentlemen upon the platform.

They will have the effect of intimidating our witnesses. Their place is with the rest of the people in the body of the hall. We have no objection to Miss Quested remaining on the platform since she has been unwell; we shall extend every courtesy to her throughout.

Mrs Turton I do wish he would just give the verdict.

Das It was only to Miss Quested that I gave permission to sit up here. Her friends should be excessively kind to climb down.

Ronny Well done, Das, quite sound.

Mrs Turton Climb down, indeed, what incredible impertinence.

Major Callender All this moving around is unhealthy in this heat.

The clatter of chairs descending from the platform, along with **Adela**, *as her light shifts with her. A cheer is raised in the gallery.* **Das** *bangs for silence.*

Das Mr McBryde . . .

McBryde Yes. I would like to deal at length with the prisoner's dupes and indeed, to show a plan of the Marabar Hills, where this dreadful deed took place . . .

On the side of the stage – a carriage on a mail train. **Mrs Moore** *is writing a letter.*

Mrs Moore I suppose I have all I wished for. I have escaped the trial, the marriage and the hot weather, and soon I will see you, dearest Ralph and Stella, but that and that alone fills me with enthusiasm. I'm afraid I have reached a state where the horror of the universe and its smallness are both visible at the same time – what can I call it? – it's a sort of twilight of the double vision in which so many elderly people like myself are involved. If this world is not to my taste, well, at all events there is Heaven, Hell, Annihilation – one or other of those large things, that huge scenic background of stars, fires, blue or black air. But in this twilight of the double vision a spiritual muddledom is set up for which no high-sounding word can be found; we can neither act nor refrain from action, we can neither ignore nor respect infinity. Oh, wouldn't it be simple – not to mention dignified – if one could be one with the universe. Ah yes. Indeed. I hesitate sometimes putting my thoughts to you, but there is something of me in the two of you, I know that, whereas I seem to be entirely absent from your half-brother.

The courtroom. The two lights persisting on **Adela** *and* **Aziz**.

McBryde *is in mid-speech.*

McBryde . . . and finally, the culminating evidence: the discovery of the field glasses on the prisoner. The prisoner is one of those individuals who have led a double life. He has been very cunning at concealing and pretending to be a respectable member of society, getting a government position even. He behaved most cruelly, brutally, to another of his guests, another English lady. In order to get rid of her and leave him free for his crime, he crushed her into a cave, among his servants. However, that is by the by . . .

Mahmoud Ali Is my client charged with murder as well as rape?

Das Mr Mahmoud Ali . . .

Mahmoud Ali Who is this second English lady?

McBryde I don't propose to call her.

Mahmoud Ali You don't because you can't, you have smuggled her out of the country; she is Mrs Moore, she would have proved his innocence, she was on our side, she was the poor Indian's friend.

Das You could have called her yourself. Neither side called her; neither must quote her as evidence.

Mahmoud Ali She was kept from us until too late – I learn too late – this is British justice, here is your British Raj. Give us back Mrs Moore for five minutes only and she will save my friend; tell me where they have put her . . .

Ronny If the point is of any interest, my mother should be reaching Aden . . .

Mahmoud Ali Imprisoned by you there because she knew the truth!

The carriage on the mail train. **Mrs Moore** *continues her letter.*

Mrs Moore In the morning I shall reach the boat. Meanwhile, we have passed a place called Asirgarh. I have never heard of it. It had large and noble bastions, and to the right of them was a mosque. And then, ten minutes later, Asirgarh reappeared. The mosque was to the left of the bastions now. The train in its descent has described a semicircle around Asirgarh. I know no one who lives there and nothing about it, but it looked at me twice and seemed to say 'I do not vanish'.

The courtroom. There is tumult from the gallery.

Mahmoud Ali I ruin my career; no matter; we are all to be ruined, one by one.

Das This is no way to defend your case.

Mahmoud Ali I am not defending a case, nor are you trying one. We are both of us slaves . . .

Das Mr Mahmoud Ali, I have already warned you, and unless you sit down, I shall exercise my authority.

Mahmoud Ali Do so; this trial is a farce, I am going! (*The sound of* **Mahmoud Ali** *handing his papers to* **Amritrao** *and walking away, calling from the doorway.*) Aziz, Aziz – farewell for ever!

Aziz, *in his spotlight, squirms. The tumult increases. The name 'Mrs Moore' is shouted outside the courtroom by the crowd, but they pronounce it Esmiss Esmoor.*

Mrs Turton What are they saying?

Major Callender Mrs Moore, I think. Most unexpected.

Mrs Turton Mr Heaslop, how disgraceful, dragging in your dear mother.

Crowd (*outside the courtroom*) Esmiss Esmoor, Esmiss Esmoor, Esmiss Esmoor . . .

Adela Ronny?

Ronny (*his face intrudes into her light*) Is it very upsetting for you?

Adela Not in the least. I don't mind it.

Ronny Well, that's good.

Adela Don't worry about me. I'm much better than I was. I don't feel in the least faint.

Suddenly the chanting stops.

Das Mr McBryde, were you to call witnesses?

McBryde Yes. I would ask Miss Quested to please give evidence.

Adela *hesitates.* **Ronny***'s hand extends into her light and grips her hand. She walks on to the platform and sits in the witness chair.*

McBryde Miss Quested, I will try not to prolong your ordeal. Was my description of Dr Aziz invitation correct?

Adela Yes, he invited us to see the caves.

McBryde And on the day, did you and Mrs Moore make the expedition with him alone, due to the sudden absence of Mr Fielding and Professor Godbole.

Adela Yes. We did.

McBryde An elephant met you at the train?

Adela Yes. It did.

McBryde And a crowd of people?

Adela Yes.

McBryde And you arrived at the caves?

Adela Yes.

McBryde And how did you find the expedition?

Adela Rather dull, actually. (*Pause.*) Disappointing. In the first cave, a match was reflected in the polished walls. That was rather beautiful.

McBryde Was that the cave that tired Mrs Moore?

Adela Yes.

McBryde And she excused herself from further explorations?

Adela Yes.

McBryde And you went then along the rocks . . .

Adela Yes.

McBryde With Dr Aziz and a guide?

Adela Yes.

McBryde To see the larger caves?

Adela Yes.

McBryde And no one else was present?

Adela No. (*Pause.*) No one else was present to my knowledge. We appeared to be alone.

McBryde Very well, there is a ledge halfway up the hill, with caves scattered near the beginning of a watercourse . . .

Adela I know where you mean.

McBryde You went alone into one of those caves.

Adela This is quite correct.

McBryde And the prisoner followed you.

She is silent.

The prisoner followed you, didn't he?

Adela May I have half a minute before I reply to that, Mr McBryde?

McBryde Certainly.

Pause.

Adela I am not . . . I am not quite sure.

McBryde I beg your pardon?

Adela I cannot be sure.

McBryde I didn't catch that answer. You are on that landing, or whatever we term it, and you have entered a cave. I suggest to you that the prisoner followed you.

She shakes her head.

What do you mean, please?

Adela No.

Das What is that? What are you saying?

Adela I'm afraid I have made a mistake.

Das What nature of mistake?

Adela Dr Aziz never followed me into the cave.

McBryde (*slams down his papers, then picks them up*) Now, Miss Quested, let us go on. I will read you the words of the deposition which you signed two hours later in my bungalow . . .

Das Excuse me, Mr McBryde, you cannot go on. I am speaking to the witness myself. And the public will be silent. If it continues to talk, I will have the court cleared. Miss Quested, address your remarks to me, and remember you speak on oath.

Adela Dr Aziz never –

Major Callender I suggest these proceedings be stopped on medical grounds.

The shadows – of the **English** *and the* **Indians** *– now loom tall. Everyone has risen in the courtroom. There is a feeling of chaos, a sense that the whole room might explode.*

Das You withdraw the charge? Answer me!

Adela I withdraw everything.

Das Mr McBryde, do you wish to continue in the face of this?

McBryde (*to* **Adela**) Are you mad?

Das Don't question her, sir, you no longer have the right.

McBryde Give me time to consider –

Amritrao You have no choice but to withdraw, lest this becomes a scandal.

Mrs Turton He shall not. Call the other witnesses. We're none of us safe. (*She forces her way into* **Adela***'s light.*) You stupid bitch!

Hands pull her back. The chaos has increased. Shadows and sounds are falling over one another.

McBryde (*trying to sound nonchalant*) Right, I withdraw.

Shouts and screams from the gallery. **Das** *pounds his gavel down. Silence.*

Das The prisoner is released without one stain on his character; the question of costs will be decided elsewhere.

Pandemonium. Suddenly the entire courtroom is brightly lit.

Das *leaves.* **Callender** *restrains* **Mrs Turton** *from lunging at* **Adela**. **Ronny** *is swept up and away by the* **English**. **Aziz** *rises.* **Rafi** *rushes in, jubilant.* **Aziz** *swoons and is caught by* **Rafi**. *He is then lifted high on the shoulders of his friends. Jubilant*

Townspeople *run to and fro. Banners appear. Flowers are thrown.* **Fielding** *is celebrating with* **Aziz**, *who now has a garland of jasmine round his neck.*

By stark contrast, **Adela** *sits alone in her chair, on the other side of the courtroom in a daze.* **Fielding** *notices her and goes to her. The* **English** *have now totally disappeared.*

Fielding Where will you go, Miss Quested?

Adela I don't know.

Fielding You can't wander about outside.

Adela I shall walk . . .

Fielding What madness. There's a riot on. Why don't you join your own people?

Adela Ought I?

Fielding You can't, it's too late, they've left. Come with me – quick – I'll put you in my carriage.

He pulls her up from the chair. **Aziz** *sees him and shouts to him.*

Aziz Cyril, Cyril, don't leave me.

Fielding I'm coming back.

Aziz Cyril . . .

Fielding *hurries* **Adela** *out of the room.* **Aziz** *is engulfed by* **Friends** *and* **Wellwishers**. *They carry him out of the room.*

The courtroom is empty. Only the **Young Man** *remains, still pulling the punkah, as if nothing has happened.*

Lights rise on **Godbole**, *sitting on the carpet.*

A **Brahman** *brings a model made of clay and places it on an altar. Clay figures stand on the model – a king and advisers and also the mother and father of the Lord.*

A cobra of papier mâché appears on the carpet. Also a wooden cradle swinging from a frame. **Godbole** *approaches the cradle with a red silk napkin in his arms. He turns to the audience.*

Godbole The napkin is God. Not that it is. Perhaps you would like me to explain. (*He turns back to the cradle. He folds the napkin into a shape which indicates a baby. He places the napkin in the cradle.*) Ah – but has a mud village or a silk napkin or an intangible spirit been born? Perhaps all three. Perhaps none. Perhaps it is foolish to search (*Pause.*) for answers.

He is once again enveloped in mist.

The College Administration Building. **Fielding** *and* **Adela**.

Adela Thank you for giving me refuge.

Fielding I had to take you out of that crowd.

Adela Have you any explanation of my extraordinary behaviour?

Fielding Have I? None. Why make a charge if you were going to withdraw it?

Adela Why indeed?

Fielding I ought to feel grateful to you, I suppose, but –

Adela I don't expect gratitude. (*Pause.*) My echo is gone. I call the buzzing sound in my ears an echo. I have been unwell ever since that expedition to the caves, and possibly before it.

Fielding What kind of illness?

Adela *touches her head at the side, then shakes it.*

Fielding That was my first thought, the day of the arrest: hallucination.

Adela Do you think that could be so?

Fielding Can you remember when you first felt out of sorts?

Adela When I came to tea with you here, I enjoyed the singing . . . but just about then a sort of sadness began that I couldn't detect at the time . . . no, nothing as solid as sadness. Living at half-pressure expresses it best. Various other things happened – it doesn't matter what, but I was under par for all of them. I was certainly in that state when I saw the caves, and it is possible I had a hallucination there, the sort of thing – though in an awful form – that makes some women think they've had an offer of marriage when none was made.

Fielding You put it honestly, anyhow.

Adela I was brought up to be honest; the trouble is it gets me nowhere.

Fielding It'll get us to heaven.

Adela Will it?

Fielding If heaven exists.

Hamidullah *enters and is very distressed to see* **Adela**.

Hamidullah Hello, my dear Fielding. We are all celebrating. Aziz is waiting. Can you join us?

Fielding At once?

Adela I hope to leave in a moment, don't let me interrupt.

Fielding The telephone lines are broken – cut, actually. Miss Quested can't ring up her friends.

Hamidullah A great deal has been broken; more than will ever be mended. Still, there should be some way of transporting this lady back to Civil Lines.

Adela I shall go to the Dak bungalow.

Fielding I have a better idea than that, Miss Quested. You must stop here at the college. I shall be away at least two days, and you can have the place entirely to yourself.

Hamidullah I don't agree at all. There might be another demonstration tonight and suppose an attack is made on the college. You would be held responsible for this lady's safety, my dear fellow.

Fielding They might equally attack the Dak bungalow.

Hamidullah Exactly. But the responsibility ceases to be yours.

Fielding She is not going to the Dak bungalow.

Hamidullah Then where is she to go? *We shall never have done with her!*

Adela I understand that I offend you . . .

Hamidullah You do not appeal to me, Miss Quested. If you had shown emotion in court, if you had broken down, if you had beaten your breast and invoked the name of God, you might have touched my imagination and generosity. But you exhibited no passion or love for those you had wronged. Truth is not truth unless it is accompanied by kindness. And more kindness. I reject your sacrifice because, though it came from your heart, it did not include your heart. (**Adela** *is stricken by his words; he looks out at the veranda.*) Well, anyway, here is our solution. Here comes the City Magistrate.

Adela At last! Will you ask him what he wants, Mr Fielding?

Fielding He wants you, of course.

Adela He may not even know I'm here.

Fielding I'll see him first, if you prefer. (**Fielding** *walks on to the veranda.*)

Hamidullah Really – need you have exposed Fielding to this further discomfort? He is far too considerate.

There is complete silence between them. **Fielding** *returns.*

Fielding He has some news for you. You'll find him on the veranda. He prefers not to come in.

Adela Yes. (*Pause.*) You have been wonderfully kind to me. (*Goes out to the veranda.*)

Fielding He has had a cable to the effect that his mother's dead.

Hamidullah Oh, really, Mrs Moore. I'm sorry.

Fielding She died on her journey.

Hamidullah The heat, I suppose.

Fielding Let us not mention this to Aziz this evening, not on his happy night. He loved her.

Adela *returns.*

Hamidullah Oh, this is unbearable!

Adela (*sits*) Ah, me!

Fielding Heaslop is waiting for you, I think.

Adela I do so long to be alone. She was my best friend, far more to me than him. I can't bear to be with Ronny. Could you do me the very great kindness of letting me stop after all?

Hamidullah Bloody hell.

A light on **Adela** *– sitting in a chair at the College Administration Building, slowly drinking a glass of water.*

On the other side of the stage – a rooftop. The **Revellers** *are lying around, under mosquito nets, looking at the stars and trying to come down after an evening of drink and the pipe.* **Aziz** *and* **Fielding** *lie next to each other,* **Fielding** *in native dress.*

Fielding Aziz, are you awake?

Aziz No, so let us have a talk. Is this not a perfect end to our celebration?

Fielding Perfect. Look at the stars.

Aziz Let us dream plans for the future.

Fielding I am useless at dreaming.

Aziz Then goodnight. (*Turns away.*) Are you content with our day's work, Cyril?

Fielding Are you?

Aziz (*turns back*) Except that I ate too much. And drank too much probably. But I do want to plan. We can spend our holidays together, can't we? Visit Kashmir, possibly Persia. I shall have plenty of money. Miss Quested will have to pay me at least twenty thousand rupees as compensation. While with me you shall never spend a single pie. This is what I have always wanted, and as a result of my misfortunes, it has come.

Adela *pours herself another glass of water.*

Fielding You have won a great victory –

Aziz Ah. I know what you are going to say next. Let Miss Quested off paying. Am I not right? I can sense it in your voice.

Fielding I *was* thinking that.

Aziz So then the English may say, 'Here is a native who has actually behaved like a gentleman.'

Fielding My dear fellow, I quite agree, she must pay all your costs, that is only fair, but do not treat her like a conquered enemy. The sum you mentioned would ruin her.

Aziz You really do think that by letting Miss Quested off easily I shall make a better reputation for myself and Indians generally. No, no, it will be put down to weakness and the attempt to gain promotion officially. I have decided to have nothing more to do with British India, as a matter of fact. I shall seek service in some independent state.

Adela *slowly drinks the water.*

Fielding In the course of a conversation with Miss Quested . . .

Aziz I don't want to hear.

Fielding Be quiet – in the course of a conversation with Miss Quested I have begun to understand her character. She is a prig, as I have always said, but she is perfectly genuine and very brave. When she saw she was wrong, she said so. In doing so, she destroyed her standing and her reputation among her compatriots. Do treat her considerately. She really mustn't get the worst of both worlds.

Adela *pours water on a cloth and presses it against her forehead.*

Aziz Not even Mogul emperors showed mercy until they received an apology.

Fielding She'll apologise if that's the problem. Look, I'll make you an offer. Dictate to me whatever form of words you like, and this time tomorrow I'll bring it back signed.

Aziz 'Dear Dr Aziz, I wish you had come into the cave; I am an awful old hag, and it is my last chance.' Will she sign that?

Adela *spills the pitcher of water. She turns her face away.*

Fielding Well, goodnight, goodnight, it's time to go to sleep after that.

Aziz Goodnight, I suppose it is. (*Pause.*) I have an idea which will satisfy your tender mind. I shall consult Mrs Moore. Her opinion will solve everything; I can trust her so absolutely.

Fielding You are so fantastic . . . Miss Quested you won't treat generously, despite the fact that she behaved decently this morning; while over Mrs Moore there is this elaborate chivalry whereas the old lady never did anything for you at all.

Aziz I have seen her but three times, but I know she is an Oriental.

Fielding Ah. Then you know what Mrs Moore would tell you. In your heart, Aziz, you know exactly what she would say. She would want you to spare the woman who was about to marry her son.

Aziz (*pause*) Indeed. (*Pause.*) Then I will spare her. (*Pause.*) I think Cyril Fielding is a very nice chap and my best friend, but in some ways a fool. (*He turns away and closes his eyes.*)

Adela *closes her eyes.*

Godbole *on the carpet. A procession is forming. His* **Students** *have taken up instruments. They play a melody.*

Godbole We gather now to prepare our ceremony. Has our God heard the melody? Perhaps. But is our song even meant for our God? And where is God Himself, in whose honour this congregation has gathered? Smothered under rose leaves, overhung by oleographs, entirely obscured, when the wind blows, by the tattered foilage of a banana. His face cannot be seen. And the inscriptions, which the poets of the state have composed, are hung high – high – where they cannot be read.

The Government College. **Fielding** *and* **Adela**.

Adela I am returning to England. Ronny has broken our engagement. Far wiser of him. I ought to have spoken myself, but I drifted on, wondering what would happen. I would willingly have gone on spoiling his life through inertia. Oh, the trouble I've brought on everyone here . . . I can never get over it. We ought never to have thought of marriage.

Fielding About marriage I am cynical.

Adela I am not. This false start has been all my own fault. I entered that cave thinking 'Am I fond of him?' Tenderness, respect . . . I tried to make them take the place of . . .

Fielding I no longer want love.

Adela No more do I. But I want others to want it. (*Pause.*) We will meet again, I hope.

Fielding We will, in England, if I take home leave, which, as a matter of fact, might happen shortly.

Adela Oh, that would be very nice. (*She smiles.*)

Aziz *and* **Fielding** *at dinner.*

Fielding I am going quite soon to England. I am only going for a little time. On official business.

Adela *– on the other side of the stage – stands by the railings on the deck of a ship, watching the water.*

Aziz Will your business leave you much spare time?

Fielding Enough to see my friends.

Aziz Will you see Miss Quested?

Fielding If I have time.

Aziz I imagine you'll enjoy that.

Fielding You have a peculiar tone of voice.

Aziz I suppose you know there is gossip about you. They say that you and Miss Quested became rather too intimate friends after the trial, that you and she have been guilty of impropriety.

Fielding They would say that.

Aziz It's all over the town and may injure your reputation. I have tried all I could to silence such a story. Even though . . .

Fielding What?

Aziz There is perhaps some truth in it? Perhaps you and Mademoiselle Adela used to amuse one another in the evening, naughty boy.

Fielding You little rotter! Well, I'm damned. Amusement indeed. Is it likely at such a time?

Aziz Oh, I beg your pardon, I'm sure. The licentious oriental imagination was at work.

Fielding You see, Aziz: the circumstances . . . also the girl was still engaged to Heaslop, also I never felt . . .

Aziz Yes, yes . . . your little rotter was out of line.

Fielding I've offended you.

Aziz Most certainly you have not.

Fielding I was unintentionally rude. Unreserved regrets.

Aziz It is nothing, we all of us make mistakes. In a friendship such as ours a few slips are of no consequence. Shall we talk about something else?

Fielding What subject?

Aziz Poetry. Let us discuss why poetry has lost the power of making men brave. My mother's father was also a poet and fought against you in the mutiny. As it is, I am a doctor, who has won a case and has three children to support. I am, I suppose, what is known as a mature man. When you knew me first, I was a child. Everyone was my friend then. The Friend: a Persian expression for God.

Aziz *looks at* **Fielding** *and then looks away.*

Adela *takes out a letter and reads it. A sea wind blows her hair.*

A shrine next to a tree. Messages are scrawled. Flowers and earthenware saucers laid as gifts. Several **Indians** *bow in front of the shrine and leave other offerings. They then move away.* **Ronny** *and* **Turton** *move out of the shadows.*

Ronny I'll be damned . . .

Turton It's the start of a cult, I'm afraid. (*Picks up a bouquet of flowers.*) Esmiss Esmoor . . .

Ronny She's still giving trouble, still mixing herself up with natives . . .

Turton It isn't her fault, dear boy, after all she's . . .

Ronny Dead? What does happen to one's mother when she dies, I wonder? Presumably she goes to heaven.

Anyhow, she clears out. (*Looks at flowers.*) Usually she doesn't become a minor god.

Turton I think after a few months it might die down.

Adela *folds the letter and puts it in her pocket. She leaves the ship's deck.*

She is enveloped in fog and disappears.

Worshippers *sing a mantra.*

Worshippers Esmiss Esmoor, Esmiss Esmoor . . . (*And then they too are enveloped by the fog.*)

A cobra – a live version of the papier-mâché cobra – jumps out of the mist and disappears.

Mau **Villagers** *carry the wooden cradle aloft on the altar, followed by the* **Students** *who are enacting the* **Band of Sweepers** *and then they too disappear.*

The mist evaporates. Mau. **Aziz** *stands in the garden by the Shrine of the Body, staring at* **Fielding** *and* **Boy**.

Aziz I have forgotten all of you. You no longer exist. (*Starts to leave.*)

Fielding I understand there's an interesting procession from the water this evening.

Aziz I wouldn't know.

Fielding Do you think they would object to English people watching the procession?

Aziz I know nothing at all about the religion here. Mau is a Hindu state.

Fielding We had a very different reception both at Mudkul and Deora; they were kindness itself at Deora.

Aziz You should never have left them.

Fielding Indeed. Come, Ralph. (*Takes the* **Boy** *by the shoulder and starts to lead him away.*)

Aziz Goodbye, Mr Fielding, goodbye, Mr Quested.

Fielding Who on earth is Mr Quested?

Aziz Do I mispronounce that well-known name? Is this not your wife's brother?

Fielding Who on earth do you suppose I've married?

Boy I'm only Ralph Moore.

Fielding Don't you know that my wife was Mrs Moore's daughter?

Aziz *blanches, then looks away.*

Fielding Perhaps this explains your odd attitude.

Aziz What is wrong with my attitude?

Fielding Your refusal to answer any of my letters.

Aziz This is a very useless conversation.

Fielding How did you ever make such a mistake? I should think I wrote you half a dozen times, mentioning my wife by name. Miss Quested? Miss Quested is our friend, she introduced us, but . . .

Aziz So there. It amounts to the same thing. You are Heaslop's brother-in-law, are you not? What does it matter to me whom you marry? Yes, yes, I made a foolish blunder. You wrote that you had married, I read no further, I had no need to. I thought you married my enemy. I thought you'd stolen my money, but it's *as if* you stole it. (*Pause.*) I read no further. (**Aziz** *walks off.*)

Godbole *on the carpet, as a statue of the God is loaded on to a litter. His* **Students** *are with him, as are some* **Villagers**.

Godbole The procession is about to begin. It is said that saints are made in the image of gods, but perhaps it is the other way round. Has not our God learned something from our local saint, he of the separated head and body? And so tonight in his honour, we will march to the prison and release a prisoner.

Aziz *enters.*

Aziz I have seen Fielding.

Godbole Excellent.

Aziz He has not married Miss Quested.

Godbole Ah no, he married the sister of Mr Heaslop. Ah, exactly. I have known that for over a year.

Aziz Why did you not tell me?

Godbole Did I not?

Aziz Your silence plunged me into a pretty pickle.

Godbole Never be angry with me. I am, as far as my limitations permit, your true friend. Besides, it is my holy festival.

Aziz *nods and walks away.*

Godbole Noise. (*Pause.*) Noise, incense on the altar, sweat, the blaze of lights, wind in the bananas, noise, thunder. Our God is born. At last, the ceremony has begun. The procession begins . . .

Godbole *dances down a pathway along with his* **Students**, *and the statue, and the napkin, as they lead a procession to the prison.*

The Government Guest House. **Aziz** *walks in and finds* **Ralph**.

Aziz How are the celebrated bee-stings?

Ralph They throb rather.

Aziz Come here, please. Allow me to look.

Ralph *goes to* **Aziz**. **Aziz** *studies his wrist.*

Aziz I have brought you some salve.

Ralph Please leave it with me. Your hands are unkind.

Aziz Certainly not. Now, do you want me to treat your stings or do you prefer an English doctor? There is one at Asirgarh, about fifty miles away. I think I had better see Mr Fielding about you; this is really great nonsense, your present behaviour.

Ralph You should not treat us like this . . .

Aziz Like what?

Ralph Dr Aziz, we have done you no harm.

Aziz Aha, you know my name, I see. Yes, I am Aziz. No, of course your great friend Miss Quested did me no harm at the Marabar.

All the guns of the state go off in the near distance. A rocket is released in the sky. The whole town has become a blur of light.

Ralph What is happening?

Aziz The procession has reached the prison. Each year they release one prisoner to satisfy the God. It is the only part of their ritual that I know or understand. (*Pause.*) I too was a prisoner.

Sounds of the **Singers** *and the* **Band** *fill the night air.*

Singers (*in the distance*)
Radhakrishna, Radhakrishna,
Radhakrishna, Radhakrishna,
Krishnaradha, Krishnaradha,
Radhakrishna, Radhakrishna . . .

Aziz I must go back now, goodnight . . . (*Holds out his hand, which* **Ralph** *takes.*) Don't you think me unkind any more?

Ralph No.

Aziz How can you tell, you strange fellow?

Ralph Not difficult, the one thing I always know.

Aziz Can you always tell whether a stranger is your friend?

Ralph Yes.

Aziz Then you are an Oriental. (*He hands the ointment to* **Ralph**.) Take this, think of me when you use it. I shall never want it back. I must give you one little present, and it is all I have got; you are Mrs Moore's son.

Ralph I am that.

Aziz Did your mother speak to you about me?

Ralph In her letters, in her letter. She loved you.

Aziz Yes, your mother was my best friend in all the world.

A wind begins to rise.

Soon it will be our monsoon, our best weather. How I wish she could have seen them, the rains. Now is the time when all things are happy, young and old. This is India. (*He smiles.*)

Godbole, *again on the strip of carpet, addresses the audience. The* **Students** *and the procession stand behind him.*

Godbole The prisoner has been released and so, too, has been something unknowable in our spirit. Later, much later, we will take the statue of the God – the napkin, the cradle – down to the water's edge, and we will throw God away. Throw God Himself into the storm. Thus He is thrown year after year, an emblem of passage, a passage not easy, not now, not here, not to be apprehended except when it is unattainable. And then the ceremony shall be over. They will take down the banners. They will take down GOD SI LOVE. And so, finally, what will it have been about, the ceremony of the God? Do you wish to know its meaning? Can you say where was the emotional centre of it – the core, so to speak? I think you cannot. How can you locate the heart of a cloud? (*Pause.*) I am – myself – most inadequate. I have said to the God, Come, come, come . . . At the same time I have tried to place myself in the position of the God and to love whomever my mind touches upon. (*Pause.*) Like that old woman. (*Pause.*) Like that wasp.

The music starts again. The **Band** *plays. The* **Singers** *sing. They dance.* **Godbole** *joins them, dancing. Then suddenly it seems that he is dancing with* **Mrs Moore**. *They seem to float above the town, and then they all – all – disappear.*

Aziz *and* **Fielding** *sit in a field.*

Fielding We leave in the morning.

Aziz I know.

Silence.

Was your trip a success?

Fielding I think not. The schools I have inspected have been most inadequate. Compared to our school in Chandrapore, certainly.

Aziz *looks at him, is about to comment, doesn't. A pause.*

Aziz I have written to Miss Quested. Thanking her for her fine behaviour two years back. It is perfectly plain to me now that she behaved well. I thought how brave she was and decided to tell her so. And I promised my children would speak of her with the greatest affection and respect.

Fielding She will be greatly pleased.

Aziz I want to do kind actions all round and wipe out the wretched business of Marabar for ever. I have been so foolish, thinking you meant to get hold of my money; as bad a mistake as the cave itself.

Fielding I wish you would talk to my wife. She too believes that Marabar is wiped out.

Aziz How so?

Fielding I don't know. Perhaps she will tell you. She won't tell me. My wife is after something. You and I are, roughly speaking, not after anything. We jog on as decently as we can, you a little in front. But my wife is not with us. Nor is her brother. They both suffer from restlessness. Not unlike their mother. They found something soothing here –

this Krishna business perhaps. They won't talk to me about this. They know I think a certain side of their lives is a mistake. That's why I wish you would talk to her.

Aziz No. I will not.

Fielding But why?

Aziz I might like her. (*Pause.*) Let's not spoil our last few minutes together.

Fielding Surely we shall see each other again.

Aziz I think not. I want you to clear out – all of you, you too. Even you. You and the Turtons and the Callenders and the Miss Dereks. Even you. My dear Cyril, you found our schools a disgrace because deep inside you think that we Indians can't do anything right without you. We go to seed without you. Yes, even you think that. No – clear out, clear out, I say. Why are we put to so much suffering? We used to blame you, now we blame ourselves, we grow wiser. Until England is in difficulties we keep silent, but in the next European war – aha, aha! Then is our time.

Fielding Whom do you want instead of the English? The Japanese?

Aziz No, the Afghans. My own ancestors.

Fielding Oh, your Hindu friends will like that, won't they?

Aziz It will be arranged – a conference of oriental statesmen. India shall be a nation. No foreigners of any sort! Hindu and Moslem and Sikh and all shall be one! Hurrah! Hurrah for India!

Fielding India a nation! Taking your seat with Guatemala and Belgium, I suppose.

Aziz (*rises, agitated*) Clear out, you fellows, double quick, I say. We may hate one another, but we hate you most. If I don't make you go, my children will. If it's fifty or five hundred years we shall get rid of you, yes, we shall drive every blasted Englishman into the sea, and then . . . (*Half kisses him.*) And then you and I shall be friends.

Aziz *walks away.*

Fielding Why can't we be friends now? It's what I want. It's what you want.

Aziz *looks at him, then shakes his head.*

Aziz No. Not yet.

Aziz *leaves.*

Fielding *looks after him, then walks away.*

Only the Shrines of the Head and Body remain.

by the same author

Rose